A Texas Cowboy's Journal

The Western Legacies Series
Published in Cooperation with the
National Cowboy & Western Heritage Museum

58

Came two miles came to North fork of
Canadian the pretiest little stream
I ever saw, runs South east affords
any quantity of water, One mile, came
to prairie overtook Smiths herd travel
Eight miles, camp on branch some
timber good grass, cam to left of road
Cattle too tired to run much tonight
boys nearly all wore out from last
nights work, passed over a rich Country
to day, Negroe soldier here grinding Coffee
Bought Mellons Corn & Peas from
some Indians to day,, night,,

Thursday Aug 13th
Had a bully time last night Cattle
Kept quiet all night, my relief was
last & the boys dident wake me until
about day for which I feel thankful
to them for I had a good nights rest
This is a beautiful country good range

A page from Jack Bailey's 1868 journal

A Texas Cowboy's Journal Up the Trail to Kansas in 1868

By Jack Bailey

EDITED BY
David Dary

TRANSCRIBED BY
Charles E. Rand

FOREWORD BY
Charles P. Schroeder

UNIVERSITY OF OKLAHOMA PRESS : *Norman*

ALSO BY DAVID DARY

The Buffalo Book (Chicago, 1974)
True Tales of the Old-Time Plains (New York, 1979)
Cowboy Culture (New York, 1981)
Entrepreneurs of the Old West (New York, 1986)
True Tales of Old-Time Kansas (Lawrence, Kans., 1987)
More True Tales of Old-Time Kansas (Lawrence, Kans., 1987)
Seeking Pleasure in the Old West (New York, 1995)
Red Blood and Black Ink: Journalism in the Old West (New York, 1998)
The Santa Fe Trail: Its History, Legends, and Lore (New York, 2000)
The Oklahoma Publishing Company's First Century: The Gaylord Family Story (Oklahoma City, 2003)
The Oregon Trail: An American Saga (New York, 2004)

Library of Congress Cataloging-in-Publication Data

Bailey, Jack, b. ca. 1831.
A Texas cowboy's journal: up the trail to Kansas in 1868 / by Jack Bailey; edited by David Dary; transcribed by Charles E. Rand; foreword by Charles P. Schroeder.
p. cm. (Western legacies series; v. 3)
Published in cooperation with the National Cowboy & Western Heritage Museum.
Includes bibliographical references and index.
ISBN-13: 978-0-8061-3737-7 (cloth)
ISBN: 978-0-8061-4647-8 (paper)
1. Bailey, Jack, b. ca. 1831—Diaries. 2. Cowboys—Texas—Diaries. 3. Cattle drives—Texas—History—19th century. 4. Cattle drives—Kansas—History—19th century. 5. Ranch life—Texas—History—19th century. 6. Texas—Social life and customs—19th century. 7. Kansas—Description and travel. 8. Missouri—Description and travel. 9. Arkansas—Description and travel. 10. Indian Territory—Description and travel. I. Dary, David. II. National Cowboy and Western Heritage Museum. III. Title. IV. Series.

F391.B2145 2006
976.4'05'092—dc22
[B]

2005050564

A Texas Cowboy's Journal: Up the Trail to Kansas in 1868 is Volume 3 in The Western Legacies Series.

The paper in this book meets the guidelines for permanence and durability of the Committee on Production Guidelines for Book Longevity of the Council on Library Resources, Inc. ∞

Contents

Illustrations

FIGURES

MAPS

Foreword

THE history of the American West conjures many images, from gallant to lonesome, majestic to desolate, based mostly in the interpretations of writers, artists, and performers of various stripes. The cowboy is often the centerpiece of these interpretations, and audiences have enjoyed the story of the cowboy for generations, regardless of its basis in truth or fiction.

Rarely do we have the opportunity to hear firsthand from someone who lived through the defining era of the American cowboy. During the brief open-range period just following the Civil War, millions of cattle were driven north from Texas to markets and shipping points in Kansas and Nebraska by adventurous men whose stories, both factual and fanciful, underlie much of our popular Western literature and entertainment. One of those men was Jack Bailey. Fortunately for us, Jack was a literate fellow who kept a journal of his days on a round-trip journey from north Texas to Kansas, delivering a herd of cattle to market in the fall of 1868. The National Cowboy & Western Heritage Museum is pleased to share that chronicle with you.

Jack was not trying to produce a dime novel or a screenplay. He was simply recording the everyday events of his life on this job he had taken against the advice of his wife and friends. He describes the hardships, the monotony, and his own second-guessing of the decision to join the drive. He also tells of the joy he finds in his surroundings, and relates the humor of his fellow trail hands. There is no mythology or concocted romance to Jack's reporting. It is life on the trail, and as such, it includes observations on the lifestyle, environment, terrain, and culture he experienced. We are now given unique insights through his documentary record.

The National Cowboy & Western Heritage Museum has a long history of telling the story of the American cowboy in all of its permutations, from harsh reality to glowing mythology. The museum shares that story with a vast audience, as the cowboy has become symbolic of America for people around the world, signifying independence, integrity, and a certain frontier chivalry. Although Jack Bailey does not present himself in heroic terms, you will certainly find those legendary "cowboy" traits in evidence in his account.

The acquisition of Bailey's journal for the museum's archival collections in the Donald C. and Elizabeth M. Dickinson Research Center marks a wonderful addition to our record of the cowboy life in a unique bygone era. We are proud to join the University of Oklahoma Press in presenting the text of the journal as part of The Western Legacies Series.

CHARLES P. SCHROEDER
Executive Director
National Cowboy & Western Heritage Museum

Preface

On the morning of October 9, 2001, Tracy "Pody" Poe awaited my arrival at the information desk at the entrance to the National Cowboy & Western Heritage Museum. Earlier, he had told me that he had a journal in which I might have some interest. As we walked down the long hallway, Poe began to tell me the family history behind the journal, which at that point I had not seen.

We sat down in the reading room of the Donald C. and Elizabeth M. Dickinson Research Center, and Poe unwrapped the journal. It looked authentic, but it was in pretty rough shape. Its spine was nearly gone. Sections of its mottled green and black cardboard covers were missing, as were the first eighteen pages of the notebook.

By now, Don Reeves, the museum's McCasland Chair of Cowboy Culture, had joined us, and we randomly read the handwritten passages in earnest. We quickly became excited about what we were reading and about the nature of the document itself: a day-by-day journal of events, dangers, and humorous anecdotes associated with a cattle drive from northern Texas to Kansas and back, kept by Jack Bailey from August 5 through November 8, 1868.

Poe wanted to sell the journal to the museum. Toward the end of October, during the authentication and appraisal process, I transcribed the journal. By the end of November, the museum's Dickinson Research Center had purchased the journal, and it became an outstanding resource of the center's collections.

Many historians agree that the myth, legend, and heroic concepts of the cowboy have their origins in the years of the open-range cattle industry during the last part of the nineteenth century, more specifically the years from 1865 to 1895. It is estimated that from 6 million to 9 million head of cattle were driven by cowboys from Texas to Kansas between 1867 and 1886. Most of these cowboys were young men in their twenties. Lonn Taylor wrote in his 1983 book, *The American Cowboy*, "Cowboying was not an old man's job, or even a middle-aged man's job, and ten years of hard riding was about all the human body could take. . . . Cowboying was almost exclusively the work of one generation: the children who were born just before the Civil War, grew to maturity in the Reconstruction South, and entered manhood in the 1870s and 1880s."[1] During the course of his three-month odyssey, the thirty-seven-year-old Bailey complained of rheumatism, pleurisy, fever, and pneumonia. He pined for his wife and boys. Relatively speaking, Bailey was an old man doing a young man's job.

1. Lonn Taylor, *The American Cowboy* (New York: Harper & Row, 1983), pp. 19–20.

Dramatic in scope and abundant in detail, the journal entries are evocative of a time long past, of the power of nature, and of a real-life occupation that would evolve into the cowboy icon of myth and reality. A good example of this is the entry for Sunday, August 30, which reads in part:

> Another Sabbath. Hope all right at home. If they are doing well it is more than we can say. Cloudy and very dark all night. Cattle a great deal of trouble. One of the coldest dampest + foggiest mornings imaginable. A severe norther up. . . . At last came up a mountain. Can see over a large scope of level prairie country. . . . Nooning on branch. While there a dark angry looking cloud came up. Heavy thunder keen lightning and such a rain. Slack up. We started. Traveled only one mile. Came another severe cloud and turned the whole heavens loose. As it were had to take up wind hard + cold from the north. Blew the rain in our faces + the cattle. As horses wont face it so we struck camp. All chilled nearly through. Just as we stoped rain came harder. Wind harder. All nearly froze. Hard work to kindle fire. Everything so thouroughly soaked with water. Plenty wood but unhandy. But we finally got a large supply of green hickory + ash wood. Built a large log heap between the two tents as close as we could without burning and . . . Bunked for the night. Let the cattle rip. I wouldent herd to night for the herd.

Preparing Bailey's text for publication required a skilled hand, and David Dary's editorial and analytical prowess is evident throughout the book. His annotations enhance our understanding of the journal entries and provide historical context. Dary retrospectively has teamed with Bailey and offered the reader an opportunity to appreciate more fully what it was to be a "cowboy" in its earliest personification, as well as what it was like to be at work on a cattle trail. An article titled "Facts for Would-Be-Cowboys" that appeared in the March 12, 1886, issue of the *Trinidad* (Colorado) *Weekly News* probably best captures the essence of the working cowboy:

> Your "outfit," or bed, clothing and equipments, will cost you half your earnings and if you smoke freely and do not try to save money, the end of the season will leave you neither richer or poorer. You will often have a wet bed and thank Heaven for getting to it wet as it is; you will eat coarse food, everything fried in lard; you will be in saddle from 12 to 18 hours a day; you will often suffer for the want of food and water during a long day's work in the hot sun; you will expose yourself to some peril of life and more of limb; you will be for much of the time as absolutely cut off from civilization as if you were on a vessel in mid-ocean; you will vow three times a day that when you strike the ranch again you will quit; you will be sore and bruised, cold at night scorched by day; wet to the skin one hour and parched with thirst the next; and

for the rest of your life you will look back to your life on the range with longing thoughts of its charms.

The National Cowboy & Western Heritage Museum and its Donald C. and Elizabeth M. Dickinson Research Center are proud to have the opportunity to share this journal with scholars, historians, and aficionados of the American West.

CHARLES E. RAND
Director, Donald C. and Elizabeth M. Dickinson
Research Center
National Cowboy & Western Heritage Museum

Introduction

THE 1868 journal of Jack Bailey surfaced in the fall of 2001 following the death in Oklahoma City of ninety-year-old Effie Bernice Minter, a retired secretary. Miss Minter, who never married, left her property to a nephew, Tracy Coy Poe, of Oklahoma City. Poe's daughter Traci Boyd found the journal while she and her father were going through the contents of Minter's home. Poe read the journal and realized its historical significance. He contacted the Donald C. and Elizabeth M. Dickinson Research Center at the National Cowboy & Western Heritage Museum in Oklahoma City, which in due course acquired the journal for its research collection.

Bailey kept his journal in a small notebook, just 7½ inches high, 6 inches wide, and less than 1 inch thick. It is similar to the ones sold in drug and general stores in the West during the late 1860s. The notebook shows its age. Its cardboard covers are heavily worn. The spine is almost worn away, and part of the front cover is missing, along with the first eighteen pages. Six sewn, folded signatures of twenty-six pages, each bound at four positions along the section folds, remain together. Aside from a few dates that are printed at the beginning of entries, everything else is written in black ink, perhaps iron gall. Bailey's writing is not small nor is it large. He consistently stays within the printed blue lines that are a little more than a quarter of an inch apart on each page. Bailey's penmanship is good, suggesting that he learned it in school.

In tracing the journal's provenance, Tracy Poe said Bernice Minter was given the journal by her father, the late Joseph Minter of Madill. This was confirmed by Joseph Minter V, a Madill attorney and relative of Bernice Minter. As the Minter family historian, Joseph Minter V said the late Joseph Minter was born October 27, 1865, at Sulphur Springs, Hopkins County, Texas, located about halfway between Dallas and Texarkana. He grew up to become a schoolteacher. Later he read law, and about 1900 he moved from Texas to Madill, Indian Territory, now Marshall County, Oklahoma. There he became the first county attorney. At some point before his death at Madill in 1929, Minter gave his daughter Bernice the journal, which he said Jack Bailey had given to him. Where and when Joseph Minter received the journal is unknown.

Jack Bailey's journal is the earliest known day-by-day account by a Texas cowboy of a cattle drive from Texas to Kansas during the period just after the Civil War. It has the added bonus of including Bailey's record of his return journey through eastern Kansas, far southwestern Missouri, northwestern Arkansas, eastern Indian Territory, and across the Red River to his home in Parker County, Texas. Bailey describes his daily activities, including trailing cattle and rounding them up after stampedes. He records the distances covered each day, the landmarks, where water was found, and the streams crossed. He tells of the men he worked with, including two black cowboys. He relates the hardships, disappointments, and joys of life on a trail drive and on the journey home, including eating and singing around the evening campfire. He mentions sleeping in tents, but provides no description or size. There are only two references to weapons. Once he fires his pistol in the air to stampede the herd, and at another point he refers to a pistol carried by another cowboy. Apparently, not all cowboys toted guns. Later accounts suggest that many trail bosses would not allow their men to carry pistols for fear that the weapons might discharge accidentally and cause the cattle to stampede.

Bailey writes candidly about his health and that of other people on the drive. At various points on the journey he complains of rheumatism, pleurisy, fever, and pneumonia. Like so many other pioneers, Bailey treated himself. He diagnosed the pain in his side as pleurisy. He notes that he and others on the drive suffered from diarrhea on two occasions, once as a consequence of eating the meat of a badly boiled yearling, and again from consuming wild berries they picked. He became ill midway in his travels to Kansas, and only then expresses second thoughts about going on the trail drive.

Bailey freely expresses his opinions of other people on the trail drive and those he meets along the way, including

Indians and black soldiers. He also expresses strong opinions about conditions as he views them in the period immediately following the Civil War. Bailey hints in his last entry, November 8, 1868, that he hopes his journal will "interest some people." Undoubtedly, he hoped his wife and family would read it, but whether he intended it to be read by others outside the family circle is not clear. Interestingly, he uses no profanity, though he does use slang words of the period.

A description of Texans in an 1874 book, *Historic Sketches of the Cattle Trade of the West and Southwest*, in many ways seems to fit Jack Bailey, though the author, Joseph McCoy, never met Bailey. McCoy was the Illinois stock raiser responsible for making Abilene the first railhead cattle town in Kansas. Concerning Texans, he wrote:

> The majority of Texans are destitute. They are, as a class, not liberally educated, and but few of them are extensive readers, but they are possessed of strong natural sense, well skilled in judging human nature, close observers of all events passing before them, thoroughly drilled in the customs of frontier life, more clannish than the Scotch, more suspicious than need be yet often easily gulled by promises of large prices for their stock; very prone to put an erroneous construction upon the acts and words of a Northern man, inclined to sympathize with one from their own State as against another from the North, no matter what the Southern man may have been guilty of. To beat a Northern man

in a business transaction was perfectly legitimate, and regarded all such as their natural enemies of whom nothing good was to be expected. Nothing could rouse their suspicions to a greater extent than a disinterested act of kindness. Fond of a practical joke, always pleased with a good story, and not offended if it was of an immoral character; universal tipplers, but seldom drunkards; cosmopolitan in their loves; in practice, if not in theory, apostles of Victoria Woodhull [the first woman to run for president, in 1872], but always chivalrously courteous to a modest lady; possessing a strong, innate sense of right and wrong, a quick, impulsive temper, great lovers of a horse and always good riders and good horsemen; always free to spend their money lavishly for such objects or purposes as best please them; very quick to detect an injury or insult, and not slow to avenge it nor quick to forget it; always ready to help a comrade out of a scrape, full of life and fun; would illy brook rules of restraint, free and easy.[1]

Much like a modern tourist, Bailey frequently compares the land he crosses in Indian Territory and Kansas with his home country in Texas. His trail drive to Kansas, unlike other drives that occurred in later years, included women and children who traveled in wagons, and the

1. Joseph McCoy, *Historic Sketches of the Cattle Trade of the West and Southwest* (Kansas City: Ramsey, Millett & Hudson, 1874), pp. 54–55.

cooking was done at times by the women and at other times by the cowboys. On later drives there was usually someone hired to do the cooking. Bailey's observations are refreshing and not only capture the flavor of trail life but also provide insights into daily life in the regions he passes through.

The names of settlements and other geographical landmarks cited in his journal make it possible to retrace Bailey's approximate route across Indian Territory, Kansas, and portions of Missouri and Arkansas, and Indian Territory once again as he returned home to Texas. Although the Journal's opening pages are missing, it is obvious that the trail drive began in north Texas and probably crossed the Red River into Indian Territory just north of the settlement of Red River Station in north-central Montague County, Texas. Red River Station, established in 1860, was located two miles south of the Red River on Salt Creek. Once across the Red River, the trail drive moves north to Fort Arbuckle, near present-day Davis, Oklahoma, and near modern Pauls Valley, and north again to modern Ponca City before entering Kansas in Cowley County, east of Arkansas City, Kansas. The route followed by Bailey is some distance east of what later became the well-known Chisholm Trail. In 1868 the Chisholm Trail had not yet become the major cattle trail to Abilene and later to Newton and Wichita, Kansas.

Bailey makes no reference to the trail-driving techniques used, but in all likelihood the cowboys were using already long tested methods. At the front were one or more point riders leading the herd. Flank riders on the sides kept the longhorns from straying. Drag riders brought up the rear and kept cattle from straggling. Riding drag was the worst position in a trail drive because of the dust kicked up by the longhorns' hooves.

In his journal Bailey does not refer to owning any of the cattle or being paid to help drive the animals north to Kansas, but he apparently was compensated for his work, because on his return journey to Texas he had money to spend. His journal is also unclear as to the size of the herd being driven north, but the partial figures he gives suggest that the herd may have numbered between fifteen hundred and two thousand cattle. After trailing practices were perfected by 1870, the normal complement of men needed to drive a herd of twenty-five hundred cattle north included a trail boss, ten cowboys, a cook, and a horse wrangler, but Bailey's trail drive took place before this became common practice. Although Bailey mentions the names of more than twenty men on the drive, who probably were cowboys, he is unclear as to how many of them were with the herd he was trailing north. Some of the cowboys he mentions are undoubtedly from other trail herds in front of or behind his herd, all heading north. He identifies one herd as being from Waco, Texas; that herd began to travel with Bailey's herd in Indian Territory.

Bailey never reached Abilene. John Adare, presumably the herd's trail boss and perhaps owner or part owner, put

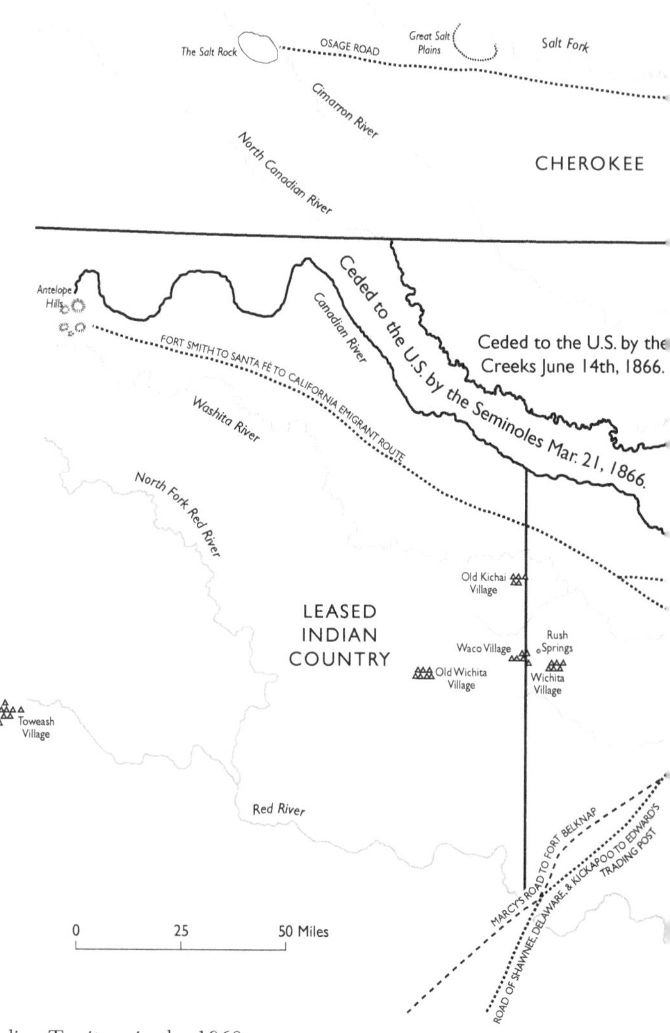

Indian Territory in the 1860s.

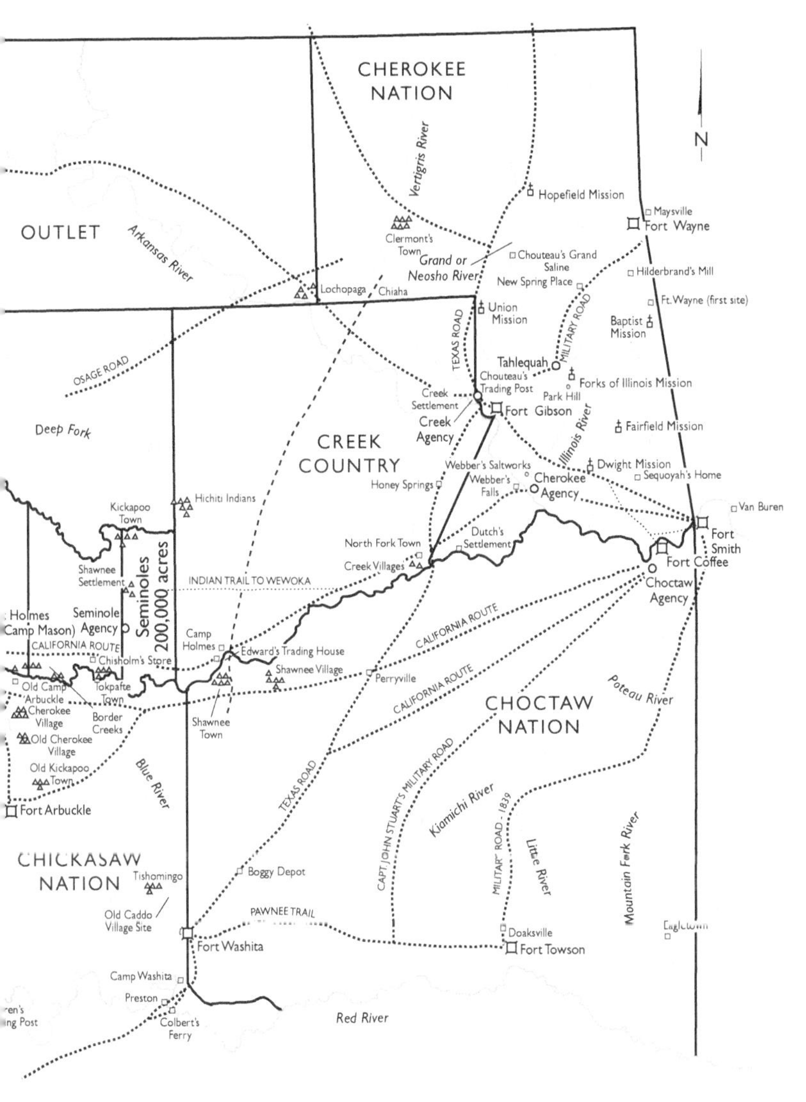

CHEROKEE NATION
N
OUTLET
Arkansas River
Vertigris River
Hopefield Mission
Maysville
Fort Wayne
Clermont's Town
Grand or Neosho River
Chouteau's Grand Saline
Hilderbrand's Mill
New Spring Place
Lochopaga
Chiaha
Union Mission
Ft. Wayne (first site)
TEXAS ROAD
MILITARY ROAD
Baptist Mission
OSAGE ROAD
Tahlequah
Chouteau's Trading Post
Forks of Illinois Mission
Park Hill
Creek Settlement
Fort Gibson
Creek Agency
Illinois River
Fairfield Mission
Deep Fork
CREEK COUNTRY
Webber's Saltworks
Dwight Mission
Webber's Falls
Cherokee Agency
Sequoyah's Home
Honey Springs
Hichiti Indians
Kickapoo Town
Van Buren
Dutch's Settlement
Fort Smith
North Fork Town
Fort Coffee
Creek Villages
Shawnee Settlement
Seminoles 200,000 acres
INDIAN TRAIL TO WEWOKA
Choctaw Agency
Holmes
Camp Mason)
Seminole Agency
CALIFORNIA ROUTE
Camp Holmes
Chisholm's Store
Edward's Trading House
Shawnee Village
Perryville
Old Camp Arbuckle
Tokpafte Town
Cherokee Village
Border Creeks
Shawnee Town
Poteau River
CHOCTAW NATION
Old Cherokee Village
Old Kickapoo Town
Blue River
Fort Arbuckle
CAPT. JOHN STUART'S MILITARY ROAD
Kiamichi River
MILITARY ROAD - 1839
Little River
Mountain Fork River
CHICKASAW NATION
Tishomingo
Boggy Depot
Old Caddo Village Site
PAWNEE TRAIL
Fort Washita
Doaksville
Fort Towson
Camp Washita
Preston
Colbert's Ferry
Red River

many cattle on shares with stock raisers in southern Kansas to fatten them for market. The smaller herd did not require as large a crew, so Bailey and a few other cowboys did not go with the cattle to Abilene. It was then that Bailey and others, including the women and children, traveled to Emporia and Lawrence, Kansas. From there Bailey and a few other cowboys started the journey back to Texas, while others, including Adare and his family, apparently remained in Lawrence for a time.

John Adare's background is not known, but several other people mentioned in Bailey's journal have tentatively been identified. Bailey wrote in his journal throughout the day, giving the reader a feeling of spontaneity that creates suspense and captures the flavor of his travels. To save space in his notebook, Bailey made ample use of abbreviations, and he used as few words as possible in recording his travels. On page 139 of his journal, Bailey wrote: "Now you have my travels to Kansas and back home. I have left out some things that I wish I had put in but my paper run short before I got to Kansas. I don't force you to read this so if you don't like it, just lay it down and don't criticize me for I make no pretintions toward writeing or any thing of the kind. Hope it will interest some people." One wishes Bailey had had more paper because he tells a good story. His spelling, grammar, and punctuation leave much to be desired. Still, there is no question Bailey was an intelligent man with some education and much common sense.

WHO WAS JACK BAILEY?

Aside from signing his name near the end of his journal, Bailey provides only a few clues as to his identity. In 1868 his home was in northeast Parker County, Texas. Bailey identifies September 14 as his birthday, but he does not list the year of his birth. The name "Jack" could be a nickname, most likely for "John." He refers to his wife, "Mat," and two boys back in Texas, presumably his sons. One he calls "Charlie boy." He mentions visiting in or near Emporia, Kansas, with Newton Nix and family, "a former neighbor in Jack County, Texas." The trail drive undoubtedly began in Texas and probably originated in one of the first three tiers of counties just south of the Red River.

Using these clues, I consulted historical books containing biographical information on early Texas cattlemen and the cattle trade, but with no success. Next I examined the 1860, 1870, and 1880 census rolls for many counties in North Texas, along with genealogical records. Because the counties in north Texas were on the Texas frontier in 1868 and plagued with Indian raids, their populations were small and easy to check. For instance, Parker County, Bailey's home in 1868, had a population of only 4,213 in 1860 and only 4,186 in 1870. Wise County had a population of 3,160 in 1860, and only 1,450 in 1870. Jack County had 1,000 residents in 1860, but only 694 in 1870. Clay County had 109 residents in 1860 and 350 in 1870, while Montague County, bordering on the Red

River, had only 849 residents in the 1860 census and 891 in 1870. Aside from a few merchants in these counties, most residents were engaged in farming and stock raising. The circumstantial evidence strongly suggests that Jack Bailey was John W. Bailey, born about 1831 in Mississippi. But his mention of his birthday as being September 14 was of no further help. Two genealogical researchers agree that John W. Bailey was born in 1831, but they do not agree on whether he was born in Alabama or Mississippi. One suggests that Bailey was born circa December 1831 but offers no documentation. Born in 1831, John W. Bailey would have been about thirty-seven when he wrote his journal.

Exactly when Bailey moved west to Texas is not known, but a John W. Bailey is listed as an original landowner in Jack County, Texas, which was established by the Texas legislature on August 27, 1856, following the arrival of the first settlers in 1855. Jack County was named for William H. and Patrick C. Jack, participants in the Texas Revolution. John W. Bailey's name appears on the 1858 and 1859 tax rolls for Jack County. Other Jack County records indicate that on June 7, 1858, Bailey married Martha A. Ham ("Mat"?), who was born July 24, 1841, in Milam County, Texas. She was the daughter of Berry Lewis Ham and Dorcas Matilda Bowen, then residing in Jack County. The 1860 Jack County census lists Bailey's occupation as stock raiser, and gives his wife's name as Martha, but lists no children.

Since Bailey returned to his home in northeast Parker County in the fall of 1868, it was thought that his name might appear in the 1870 Parker County census rolls. It does not. Likewise, a check of the 1870 census rolls for Jack and other nearby counties does not list John W. Bailey or his wife. However, the 1880 census of Jack County, Texas, lists John W. Bailey, occupation farmer, his wife Martha, and four children (three boys and a girl), though no child named Charlie. The 1880 census identifies the children as M. B. (Beulah) Bailey, age ten; A. A. Bailey, age eight; Henry Bailey, age six; and Jack Bailey, age three. Bailey's journal reference to his two boys, including "Charlie boy," raises the possibility that both children may have died young, because in the 1880 census Bailey's oldest child was only ten, having been born in 1870, two years after Bailey wrote his journal.

The 1880 Jack County census, however, does list a John C. (Charles?) Bailey as a neighbor to John W. Bailey. John C. Bailey was then twenty-four. His wife's name was Mary, and they had three children: Mary E., age five; Nora E., age two; and Alpha, one year. John C. Bailey might be the missing "Charlie boy," but the 1880 census lists his place of birth as Missouri and his parents' places of birth as Illinois. If accurate, this information would eliminate John C. Bailey, born in 1856, three years before John W. Bailey married Martha Ham. If the 1880 census information on John C. Bailey is not accurate, it raises the possibility that Martha Ham was John W. Bailey's second wife and that Bailey lived in Missouri before moving to Texas, where he remarried. The 1850 Missouri census, however, does not list a John W. Bailey or a John C. Bailey. If John C. Bailey was John W. Bailey's son, he would have been twelve years old in 1868.

The evidence favoring John W. Bailey as Jack Bailey is much stronger when we consider other references in his journal. For example, he frequently refers to another cowboy on the drive named Bud Ham, who appears to have been Bailey's brother-in-law. Berry Lewis Ham and Dorcas Matilda Bowen, the parents of Bailey's wife, Martha, had fourteen children. Martha, born in 1841, was the second oldest child. The third oldest was Abner Lewis Ham, born May 26, 1843, in Milam County, Texas. Family records indicate that Abner's nickname was "Bud." In 1861, when he was nineteen, he began service as a Texas Ranger. His service ended in 1863. In 1868, the year of the trail drive, he was twenty-five. Genealogical records indicate that he married twice and that he died in Tulsa, Oklahoma, in 1927 at the age of eighty-three.

Bud and Martha's father also had a colorful background. Berry Lewis Ham was born in Tennessee in 1812 and moved to Texas during the 1830s. He fought in the Texas Revolution as a soldier in the Republic of Texas army. He was one of the men who tried unsuccessfully to rescue Cynthia Ann Parker after she was taken captive by Indians in May 1836 in what is now Parker County, Texas. He lived in several areas of Texas until the 1850s, when he settled eight miles west of Jacksboro,

Jack County, Texas. John W. Bailey and his wife, Martha, were Ham's neighbors in 1860, according to that year's census.

In his journal Bailey tells of visiting with Newt Nix and family in the vicinity of Emporia, Kansas, while on the journey. Bailey notes that Nix was a former neighbor of his in Jack County, Texas. The 1858 and 1859 tax rolls in Jack County, where John W. Bailey's name appears, also contain the name "Newton Nix," and the 1870 census for Lyon County, Kansas, confirms that a Newton Nix and his wife and children were living in the Emporia area.

John W. Bailey's name appears in the 1880 Jack County census. He was then forty-eight. It seems likely that he lived in Jack County until the early 1890s. His wife, Martha A. Bailey, died at the age of fifty on March 23, 1891, in Jack County, Texas, and is buried there in the Ham Cemetery. John W. Bailey's name does not appear again until mid-1899, when he applied for a Confederate pension soon after the Texas legislature on May 12 agreed to provide pensions to any indigent soldiers or sailors of the Confederacy. In his application, preserved in the Texas State Archives, Bailey listed his age as sixty-nine and stated that he had been a resident of the town of Israel, Freestone County, Texas, southwest of Dallas, since 1895. He listed his occupation as farmer, but claimed that he was unable to perform manual labor because of old age and general debility. He listed his personal property as one horse valued at fifteen dollars.

In his pension application, Bailey noted that he had served in Company F, 31st Mississippi Regulars, volunteers, during the Civil War. This suggests that Bailey was a native of Mississippi and that he returned there at the start of the Civil War. Bailey's application, dated July 8, 1899, was approved, but what happened to him after 1899 is not known. When and where he died remains a mystery.

HISTORICAL BACKGROUND

Drives of Texas cattle to northern markets began before the Civil War. The earliest known drive took place in 1846, when Edward Piper, an eastern cattle buyer, acquired a thousand Texas longhorns and drove them to Ohio. Unfortunately, if Piper kept a diary or journal, it has not been found. Between the late 1840s and the Civil War other Texans drove herds of longhorns across Indian Territory into southeastern Kansas Territory and Missouri, where the cattle were either sold or shipped east by railroad to markets.

Tom Candy Ponting made the first cattle drive from Texas to Missouri of which something is known. Ponting and a partner went to northeastern Texas in 1853, bought more than seven hundred head, and started north across eastern Indian Territory. There they purchased a few more cattle before continuing their drive into southeastern Missouri and east into Illinois. Years later Ponting wrote three articles describing his journey that were published in the *Decatur* (Illinois) *Review* in 1907. Herbert O. Brayer later used the articles in writing his *Life of Tom Candy Ponting, An Autobiography*, published in 1952.

The earliest known diary of a trail drive from Texas north was kept by George Duffield in 1866, two years before Jack Bailey made his journey. Duffield, a Burlington, Iowa, businessman, heard that Texas cattle were plentiful and cheap. He and a partner, Harvey Ray, went to Texas, where they purchased about a thousand longhorns near Austin and drove them north to Ottumwa, Iowa. Duffield's diary is preserved and was reprinted in a journal, *Annals of Iowa,* in 1924. But it contains little detail of the drive, only short summaries of each day's activities probably entered at the end of each day. Jack Bailey's journal gives a far more vivid picture than Duffield's diary, especially given that Bailey made his entries throughout the day whenever he had spare time. Then, too, Bailey's journal captures his personal experiences and his reflections on the country he crossed, the people he traveled with and met along the way, and his own thoughts.

One year before Jack Bailey made his trail drive north, the new settlement of Abilene became the first Kansas railhead cattle town on the Union Pacific Railroad, Eastern Division, line west of Kansas City, Missouri. To the south in Texas, there was an overabundance of cattle. Texan stock raisers returning home following the Civil War found their cattle had multiplied on the open ranges. Many old men and young boys who had been left to care for the cattle during the war had neglected their jobs.

Artist J. Andre Castaigne's depiction of a western cattle roundup appeared in *Scribners* magazine in June 1892. Courtesy Kansas State Historical Society, Topeka.

Then, too, during winter storms in 1862 and 1863 many cattle had been scattered. Thus, when the Civil War ended in 1865, there were so many cattle in Texas that their value had dropped to one or two dollars a head, and that price depended upon finding a buyer.

Cattle were then just about the only thing of value in Texas. Stock raisers in need of money began cow hunts to find their cattle and then to locate markets for their animals. Some cattle were driven to New Mexico, while others went to markets in Louisiana or were sold at low prices to the Morgan Steamship Company in Indianola or Galveston along the Texas coast. The Morgan company then shipped the cattle to New Orleans and Cuba, where the animals were sold for a handsome profit. Other Texans found they could sell their cattle for the animals' hides, bones, tallow, and horns. Hide and tallow factories were established at Rockport and Fulton, Texas, and the by-products were shipped by boat to New Orleans and elsewhere.

After learning that sirloin steaks were selling for twenty-five to thirty-five cents a pound in New York City, Texans again began to eye northern markets. In 1866 an estimated 250,000 head of Texas cattle were driven north across eastern Indian Territory toward southeastern Kansas and Missouri, but only half of them reached their destinations because of what was then called the "Spanish Fever." When Texas cattle trailed north to Kansas and Missouri came into contact with settlers' cattle, the domestic animals came down with "Spanish Fever." This began occurring during the 1850s. Missourians called the disease "Texas Fever." It was a splenetic fever caused by ticks carried by the longhorns, though the cause was not identified until several years later. The ticks sometimes made longhorns sick, but these hardy animals did not die from the disease. Domestic cattle in Missouri and Kansas did.

In 1855 the Missouri legislature passed a law making it illegal for drovers from outside Missouri to drive diseased cattle into the state. Then in 1859 the Kansas legislature passed a law barring all Texas, Arkansas, and Indian cattle coming from Indian Territory from entering the four organized Kansas counties along the southeastern border of Kansas between June 1 and November 1.

In 1866 Texans began driving their herds across the Red River at Preston, Texas, and then northeast over the Shawnee Trail. Along the border of southeast Kansas and southwest Missouri, most herds were turned back by armed settlers. On February 16, 1867, Governor Samuel J. Crawford of Kansas signed a new law that prohibited the driving of Texas or Indian cattle into Kansas between March and December *except* west of the Sixth Meridian and south of a line running from northeast of modern McPherson, Kansas, west to the Colorado border. The law opened a large piece of unsettled land in south-central and southwest Kansas to Texas cattle traffic twelve months a year. The law said that any person, association, or company could select a route through this region to some point on the Union Pacific Railroad, Eastern Division. There longhorns could be shipped out of the state. The law also required posting of a ten-thousand-dollar bond by the drover to ensure payment of any damages caused by Texas cattle.[2]

In the spring of 1867 far fewer cattle were driven up the Shawnee Trail to Kansas and Missouri than in 1866. Many stock raisers, however, began to gather their herds in Texas in hopes that new markets would develop in that area of Kansas where Texas cattle could be trailed throughout the year. Some Texans decided to drive their

2. *Laws of Kansas*, 1867, Sess. 7, pp. 263–67.

herds of longhorns north in hopes of finding a market, and before 1867 ended, thirty-five thousand cattle were sold in Abilene, Kansas. Joseph McCoy wrote that the first herd to arrive at Abilene in 1867 had been driven north by a Texan named Thompson, who sold the herd in Indian Territory to Smith, McCord & Chandler, a partnership of three northern men. They took the herd to Abilene and sold it. Three Californian partners named Wheeler, Wilson, and Hicks bought a herd of longhorns in Texas and drove them north into Kansas, where they planned to turn west and sell the cattle in California. They camped about thirty miles from Abilene to rest their animals. After being told that Abilene was a cattle market, they sold their cattle there.

Bailey's journal strongly suggests that many Texas stock raisers learned of Abilene by the spring of 1868 because of steps taken by McCoy beginning in the fall of 1867. McCoy realized that he needed to publicize Abilene if more Texas cattle were to be driven there, sold, and shipped east by train. During that winter he had circulars mailed to every Texas stock raiser whose address had been obtained the previous summer, inviting them to bring their herds of marketable cattle to Abilene. Many Texas newspapers reprinted the circulars, giving the information wide coverage. Gradually the word spread. McCoy and others promoting Abilene also spent a reported five thousand dollars in advertising the railhead markets in every publication read by northern cattle buyers. Meantime, construction of the Drover's Cottage, a hotel in Abilene, was completed to house drovers and buyers.

When the spring of 1868 arrived, cattle buyers began gathering in Abilene about a month before the first Texas herds arrived. That year at least seventy-five thousand Texas cattle arrived in the town, including those driven by John Adare that had not been put on shares with Kansas stock raisers in southern Kansas. Although several Texas stock raisers are mentioned in McCoy's book, there is no mention of John Adare or the cattle he sold in Abilene in 1868—probably because his herd was small in comparison to others.

By the summer of 1868, as Jack Bailey and others were trailing their herd north, McCoy realized that a more direct trail was needed from southern Kansas to Abilene. He sent men south to survey a route from Abilene to where Wichita, Kansas, stands today, a distance of ninety miles. That route was considerably to the west of the route followed by John Adare in driving his remaining cattle to Abilene in 1868. McCoy's men marked the new route by erecting small mounds of earth. This may have been the first time in history when a cattle trail was laid out with some mathematical precision.

Bailey's reference to other Texas cattle herds in front of and behind the herd he was trailing strongly suggests that McCoy's publicity had worked, but the route followed by drovers in 1868 was far to the east of what would become the Chisholm Trail. The route followed by Bailey and others was seemingly used for only two or three years—not long enough for it to be called anything more than a trail to Kansas. It was not the Chisholm Trail. The earliest known reference to the Chisholm Trail in print appeared in the *Kansas Daily Commonwealth*, Topeka, on May 27 and October 11, 1870. Later Texas newspapers referred to cattle following the Chisholm Trail. The *Daily News* published at Denison, Texas, made reference to Texas cattle going up "the famous Chisholm Trail," in a story published April 28, 1874.

Not surprisingly, Bailey makes no reference to himself as a "cowboy" on the trail drive. The word "cow-boy," the natural combination of the words "cow" and "boy," began to come into use only during the late 1860s in the American West. "Cow-boy," however, dates back to Ireland in about A.D. 1000, when horsemen and cattle wranglers became known as cow-boys. During the seventeenth century, when England was trying to populate the American colonies, some Irish cow-boys fell into disfavor with the British rulers and were given a choice between jail and America. Many chose America, where they were indentured to farmers for work and keep. It is no wonder that stock raisers in the colonies shunned the "cow-boy" label and adopted the English term "drover" as their occupational title when driving cattle to market. The word "cow-boy" was not held in high regard during the American Revolution, when Loyalist guerrillas calling themselves "cow-boys" stole cattle from American farmers and sold them to the British. "Cow-boy" did not come into common use in the United States until after

Jesse Chisholm, for whom the Chisholm Trail is named. The trail, located some distance west of the route followed by Jack Bailey, was only in its infancy in 1868. Courtesy Kansas State Historical Society, Topeka.

eastern writers discovered the strangely dressed and often armed men on horseback trailing Texas longhorns north to the railhead cattle towns of Kansas. It was not until about 1900 that the hyphen was dropped, creating the word "cowboy."

In 1869, the year following Bailey's journey north, increasing numbers of drovers gathered their herds in Texas and drove them north to Abilene. By then Texans realized that Abilene was not a northern swindle, and by the fall of 1869 more than 350,000 head had reached the Abilene area. Not all of them were shipped east by railroad. Some were trailed farther north and west to stock new ranches in Colorado, Wyoming, Nebraska, and elsewhere. Other drovers were attracted to alternate shipping points on what was then called the Kansas Pacific. (The Union Pacific Railroad, Eastern Division, changed its name to Kansas Pacific on May 31, 1868.) Still other drovers trailed their cattle north of Abilene to Waterville, Kansas, the western terminus of the Central Branch Railroad. In 1870 the same number of longhorns was trailed from Texas to Abilene as in 1869, but 1871 found twice as many cattle, more than 700,000 head, driven north to Kansas. That was Abilene's biggest year as a cattle-trading center. It was also the town's last.

The townspeople of Abilene realized that the ever increasing number of farmers around their town provided year-round business and created a stable economy, while the Texas trade was seasonal. Moreover, the unsavory characters attracted by the cattle trade often carried off much of the money spent or lost by the cattlemen, drovers, and cowboys. Early in February 1871 Theodore C. Henry, who from 1869 to 1871 had served as Abilene's first mayor, wrote copy for a circular to which four-fifths of the citizens of Abilene signed their names. The circular asked that Texas cattle be driven elsewhere because the residents of Abilene and surrounding Dickinson County would no longer submit "to the evils of the trade." Copies of the circular were distributed south from Abilene into Indian Territory and Texas. Texas cattle did not return to Abilene, but the circular was not the cause. A few weeks after it had been printed, the Kansas legislature in March 1872 pushed the quarantine line farther west, making it illegal to drive longhorns to Abilene. By then other Kansas towns were seeking to capture the cattle trade.

The Kansas legislature changed the quarantine line four more times—in 1876, 1877, 1879, and 1883—each time pushing it farther west. Each time the line was moved, existing cattle towns died and new ones sprang up. In 1885 the Kansas legislature banned any Texas cattle from being trailed anywhere in Kansas. By then, however, railroads had begun to penetrate Texas, pretty much eliminating the need for cattle drives to Kansas and elsewhere. The cattle towns of Baxter Springs, Coffeyville, and Chetopa, all located in southeast Kansas on the border with Indian Territory, survived the quarantine laws of the 1870s and early 1880s by building cattle pens just across the border in Indian Territory. Texas cattle would be held in Indian Territory until they were sold.

They were then loaded aboard railroad cars and shipped through eastern Kansas. The quarantine laws did not prohibit shipping Texas cattle through Kansas by rail, only driving the animals overland.

Kansas communities that served as cattle towns for brief periods included:

Abilene, 1867–71
Waterville, 1868–69
Junction City, 1869–70
Chetopa, 1869–74
Coffeyville, 1869–73
Newton, 1871
Salina, 1869–71
Solomon, 1869–71
Ellsworth, 1871–75
Brookville, 1871
Wichita, 1872–76
Great Bend, 1871–75
Caldwell, 1880–85
Dodge City, 1877–85

There is no question that the cattle towns influenced the material culture of the Texas cattlemen, drovers, and cowboys. For some, the experience may have changed their views of people in other occupations or simply reinforced them. For the cattlemen, the cattle towns provided long-sought-after markets for their Texas cattle and profits that made some of them cattle barons. Their new wealth enabled many Texans to improve their standard of living, to travel, and to do all the things wealthy people did during the late nineteenth century. For the drovers and cowboys, the cattle-town markets created jobs driving the herds to Kansas. These men were paid for their work, and many spent all or most of their wages on new material possessions or fun in the cattle towns, or both. Merchants, saloonkeepers, gamblers, prostitutes, and other people in the cattle towns benefited materially. They in turn provided new experiences for the Texans.

Certainly, the Kansas cattle towns and the railroads saved the Texas cattlemen from ruin, but they also brought change. The cattle towns were mixing places for different types and classes of people from different geographic regions. However, the railroads that helped to create the Kansas cattle towns and brought the material goods that were sold to the Texans also carried settlers. Most of these settlers were farmers determined to build their homes on the plains and prairies, and to till the land that was being grazed or crossed by the Texas longhorns. They did not understand the Texas cattlemen, drovers, and cowboys or their system of cattle raising. Many Texans viewed the settlers as interlopers. Yet the law was on the side of the settlers. Most lawmakers in Washington did not understand the cattlemen's western system of cattle raising, which was tied to the semi-arid conditions of the plains from Texas to Canada. The eastern laws relating to land and water rights were satisfactory in the East, but they were unsuited to the needs and conditions of the cattlemen in the West. As settlers, backed by the law, pushed across the central plains, cattlemen began either to adjust or else to seek new regions where the grass was a little greener and eastern ways had not yet arrived.[3]

3. David Dary, *Cowboy Culture: A Saga of Five Centuries* (New York: Alfred A. Knopf, 1981), pp. 168–97.

A Texas Cowboy's Journal

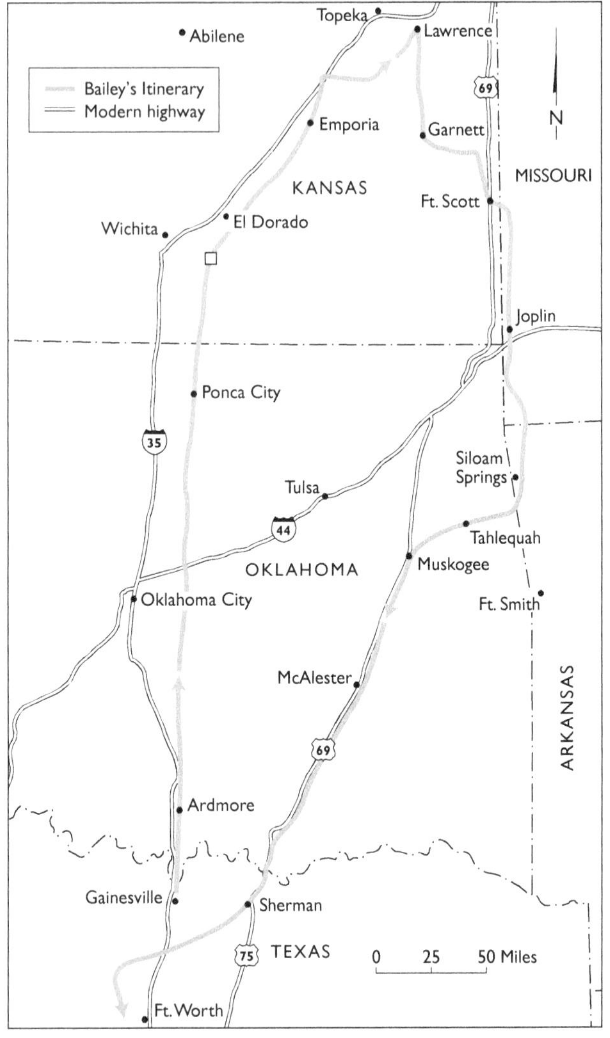

A modern map showing the approximate route followed by Jack Bailey. The point marked with a square to the east of Wichita in what is today Cowley County, Kansas, indicates where the cattle herd was held.

Jack Bailey's Journal

EDITOR'S NOTE

In his transcription of Jack Bailey's journal, Charles E. Rand chose to retain Bailey's often phonetic, original spelling. In some cases words were unrecognizable, even given a context. In these instances Rand spelled the word the way he saw it and added "[*sp?*]" beside it to indicate a probable spelling error. Bailey used a plus symbol (+) in place of the word "and." Bailey also used the letters "ms" as his abbreviation for "miles." He used punctuation marks and capitalization somewhat randomly. Words that Bailey underlined for emphasis appear here as underlined. In this edited version, Bailey's spelling, use of datelines, and lack of paragraphing have been retained. His original pagination is given in italics in square brackets (e.g., [*page 4*]). In some instances missing letters and words have been inserted in brackets for the sake of clarity. In addition, periods have been inserted to mark the end of sentences, and the first letter of the first word of each sentence has been capitalized to facilitate reading and understanding. Commas have not been added. Ellipses in square brackets (e.g., [...]) indicate text lost due to a missing portion of a page.

The first eighteen pages of the journal are missing. The journal begins on Tuesday, August 5, 1868, several days after the herd crossed the Red River into Indian Territory from Texas.

[*page 19*] Best place to water cattle + horses we have come to yet. Travel up the creek one mile. Come to a large spring which makes the creek. Rise a mountain. Come on to prairie. High dry + rocky. Very broken. I am on a very high peak. Can see the cattle drinking + travel leasurely along the branch or creek. I set up a long rock 2 feet on end put my name on it. Can see the rock one mile or more. Rang[e] is tolerable good. Dont Sanders was runing a cow today. She fell + broke her leg. Had to leave her. 2 oclock start. I + Bud pointing herd to day. Negroe Soldier passed us to day with team going to Arbuckle. We have stoped now to let the tail end of herd catch up. They are 2 miles back. Country is improveing in looks. Crossed water twice since diner. Camp at a place. Not much water. [*page 20*] Half mile back was a splendid place to camp. We are in a beautiful little grove. Water scarce + muddy, bad herding ground. Traveled 10 ms to day. We are in 4 miles of Arbuckle. Can see little Indian farms scatered around sounding. Up herd for the night. We are on the waters of buchita River.[1]

1. The "buchita" River is probably the Washita River, which rises in northwest Texas and flows east into Oklahoma and then southeast to south-

Wednesday Aug 5th 1868

Cattle herded fine last night. A Negroe came to camp last night to trade dry cows for cows + calves fixing to start. Gus is better this morning. He is mending since I took him in charge. Had roasting years for breakfast this morning. Course leads off East of North. Left camp 8 oclock. Just after leaving camp I swaped Beans more [mare?] to a Negroe for a paceing horse. Made an excelent trade. [*page 21*] We are watering the cattle now ½ [?] Mile from Arbuckle in a spring. Prairie branch. No timber on it. Water very shallow but plenty for a herd of cattle. We can see the US flag, the stars + stripes, once the proudest emblems of any nation under the canopy of heaven, now floating over the heads of a Company of flat nosed ignorant negroes, claiming to be a protectors of that flag an the country once a free country now monarchy, tyrany, treachery, and everything that is low

---

central Oklahoma. Bailey makes no reference to what he saw in the river, but about fifty miles southeast of where he crossed the stream, alligators could be found in the Washita River. O. H. Todd and other members of a party surveying the Chickasaw Nation reported seeing them during this period. If Bailey had seen alligators, he would undoubtedly have made a note of it in his journal. Bailey's reference to Arbuckle indicates that on August 4 the cattle drive was near Fort Arbuckle, which is located about seven miles west of modern Davis, Oklahoma, and just south of Oklahoma State Highway 7. Fort Arbuckle, the fourth military post constructed in Indian Territory, was established in the spring of 1851. The fort consisted of several sturdy log buildings near a crossing on the Washita River. In 1868 Gen. Philip Sheridan made Fort Arbuckle the supply center for his Indian campaign, and large quantities of grain and hay were collected there. But in 1869 the soldiers were moved to Fort Sill and Fort Arbuckle was abandoned.

and degradeing governed by Negroe Supremacy [...] Enough [...][2]

Pasing over a beautiful country owned by the Chickasaw Indians. Beautiful groves + scirt- of timber + some very pretty little farms. Passed through the fort about 11 oclock. Came out 2 ms. Stoped to noon at a branch. An old half breed woman has been following us all day claiming a steer that she knows don [*page* 22] belong to her but to get rid of her Adare finally gave her up and partly through fear.[3] She made some very strong threats if she dident get him [the steer] so she got him. Adare met an old negroe acquaintance invited him to take diner with him. He + the old Negroe sat down together to eat a hearty meal sold the old devil a good cow for $7.00 in currency. Rested 2 hours. Started. Course nearly

2. The black soldiers at Fort Arbuckle were Buffalo Soldiers of the 10th U.S. Cavalry, formed at Fort Leavenworth, Kansas, in 1866. They were named "Buffalo Soldiers" by the Cheyenne and Comanche Indians against whom they fought. The sight of black American soldiers garrisoning a U.S. fort may have reminded Bailey of the policies of Reconstruction. These were being imposed by Radical Republicans, who dominated the U.S. Congress and sought to punish former Confederate states including Texas following the Civil War. Texas Republicans were known as "radicals." Emancipation changed the labor system, and the end of slavery forced a redefinition of the relationship between blacks and whites.

3. Adare is John Adare, apparently the trail boss and possible owner or part-owner of the herd. His wife, identified only as Mrs. Adare, mentioned later as being on the drive along with other women and children, is sometimes referred to as the "old lady." In a couple of places Bailey seems to use the nickname for John Adare and not his wife. The women and children apparently traveled in at least two wagons that accompanied the drive.

east. Came 2 miles. Got to Ouchita River.[4] Plenty of water. Had trouble geting through the bottom. Cattle got scared at some Negroe teamsters. Got them out though with little or no loss. Came out one + a half miles. Stoped on a lake to left of road. Grass bad wood scarce. A beautiful rich valley + a pretty lake this evening. We met a negroe sergent. I have just got to camp. Been on herd this evening. [*page* 23] The lake is about ½ mile long one hundred yds wide about 4 feet deep sandy bottom. Some of the boys are in it. The water is very clear but has a bad taste and is full of little insects. Women geting supper. Children playing on bank of lake. Martin + Frank fishing. I + Bud Ham lying on a pallet. Bud deviling Tisha (his little girl).[5] I am writeing. We have traveled up Ouchita [Washita] part of this evening over the pretiest valley of land I ever saw.[6] Eating supper, so I close for to day. Boys herding in cattle for the night. More anon

Tuesday [Thursday] August the 6th /68

Left camp 8 oclock. Traveled up Ouchita [Washita] six miles. Nooned in valley one mile from Water. Had to carry water in buckets, which is no easy job. This is an excelent country of land, [*page* 24] Chocolate color.

4. Ouchita is apparently yet another spelling for the Washita River.

5. Bailey's wording suggests that Bud Ham had his daughter and perhaps wife along on the trail drive. This is the only such reference in the journal.

6. The beautiful valley was probably in the vicinity of modern Wynnewood, Oklahoma. The lake has not been identified.

"Herd Swimming a River," by J. Andre Castaigne (*Scribner's* magazine, June 1892). Crossing streams was always a hazard on trail drives. Courtesy Kansas State Historical Society, Topeka.

Water is very scarce along the road. Fine timber, good grass. Annie is sick today. Has an attack of cramp colic. Hope nothing serious. Nothing of note hapened to day. Gus is still improveing. Is able to ride horse back this evening. Start 2 oclock. Course leads off north. Crose a creek 5 ms from Cherokee Town.[7] Creek is rather a curiosity. It has tolerable steep banks. Plenty of timber on it. Is very wide and hasent a drop of water in it. The bed is covered with beautiful white Sand. Camp near

7. In 1868 Cherokee Town was located approximately two miles east of modern Pauls Valley, Oklahoma. It was first settled in the early 1850s and took its name about 1864 after a group of Cherokee Indians, refugees from the Civil War, settled nearby.

Cherokee Town, to right of road ½ miles. No water nearer than one mile. Have to carry again in buckets. While watering the cattle this evening they kept walking down the river in the water and the timber was so thick that it was hard to get around them. Finally I galoped in a head of them + shot [*page 25*] my sixshooter right ahead of them and stampeded them. I never heard such a roar in my life, but by the time they got to where they could get out their scare got over. So nothing serious happened. I know they would run. Some Seminole Indians tryed to get Beans pony, but we wouldent give him up so they left us.[8] The cattle are very hungry tonight. Grass has not been good this evening, would not stop to graze. Gerard going out for the night.

Friday Aug the 7th 1868

Had to go for water this morning so breakfast will be late..late to start. Course bears more east this morning. Pass Shirleys tradeing house or Cherokee Town. There is a few Indians and a Negroe Company are stationed here for protection. The infernilest humbug I ever saw or heard of. [*page 26*] Crossed Sand Creek 2 ms this side

8. The cowboy named Bean, later referred to as "Bean from Cook County," may have been twenty-five-year-old J. G. Bean whose father probably was Robert Bean of Cooke County, Texas. Robert Bean laid out a wagon road with Jesse Chisholm in 1832 from Fort Smith to Fort Towson, Indian Territory. This is the same Jesse Chisholm for whom the Chisholm Trail was named. Following the 1868 trail drive, Bean apparently moved to Parker County, Texas, where his name appears on the 1870 census listing his occupation as "cow driver." Bailey refers frequently to Bean throughout the journal.

of Town. No water. Stoped in prairie. Some of the men hunting for water. Came to Indian house. I bought some watermelons. Appearance of rain. Annie is still sick but better. Dud Rogers stood my guard last night.[9] Bud Ham lost my pipe. To day got me another in Cherokee Town. We passed a herd of cattle this morning or camped near them last night. Belonging to Smith + Gholston of Waco.[10] Herd small. All Beef.[11] Two of the Lemley [Temley?] Boys are with them as hands. Boys not found water yet. Heard of some 4 ms ahead. Start for it though it is very late. Come to find out there is plenty of water one mile from road but it is too handy. Find plenty water in spring creek in holes. Our camp is ½ mile to right of road. [*page* 27] Cattle are vey dry. Traveled north to day came 7 ms.

Saturday Aug 8th 1868

Cattle hard to herd last night. Had a very bad place to herd in. Lay up to day to kill a beef. The women washing. I

9. Dud Rogers may be William Rogers, the oldest son of James Rogers, a farmer in Wise County, Texas, who was twenty-four in 1868. He is listed on the 1860 Wise County census.

10. J. R. Smith may be the Smith of Smith & Gholston of Waco, Texas. He was a prominent stock raiser in the Waco area. He came to Texas from Alabama. In 1868 Smith would have been forty-nine. Gholston may be Moses Goldstein, who moved to Waco in 1868. It was not uncommon for cowboys trailing herds close together to visit each other's camp.

11. "All beef" means there were no cows and calves in the herd. All the cattle would have been steers (that is, castrated males). During the period from 1866 to about 1870, trailing cows and calves to market was not uncommon. After 1870 Texans found that cattle buyers in the railhead Kansas cattle towns preferred steers.

The business section of Waco, Texas, in 1865, three years before Jack Bailey made his trail drive north to Kansas. According to Bailey in his journal, at least one herd of Texas cattle from the Waco area traveled north in 1868. Courtesy Kansas State Historical Society, Topeka.

shot [shod?] my horse this morning. Gus is still improveing. Annie is a good deal better this morning. A man at camp hunting oxen. Herding in for the night..got to Supper..

Sunday Aug the 9th

Had a stampede last night though nothing serious. Got them stoped. Had rain last night. Camped in sight of Smith's herd. I came on to the Canadian River this morning about 6 miles a head of herd to see if it is fordable. About knee deep. A fellow named White has a little tradeing hous here. [*page* 28] I am siting on a beautiful sand beach. Cattle have caught up with me. Are in the

River watering. River divides the Chickasaws + Creeks it is about 400 yds wide very little timber on it.[12] It is a pretty a stream as I ever saw, Indians crossing continually. Suppose they are Seminole. There is no quick sand at this time, but the Indians tells us at times it is very bad. We stop on bank to noon. No coffee no nothing for me. While I am writeing I see six or seven Indians comeing towards me. They ride good ponies. They have nothing to say, all looking at me write. Well boys are starting the herd. Our course to day is nearly north. Came 5 ms. Camp at the Seminole Church, A large spring or hole in head of Ravine, difficult to get too. [*page* 29] Bud haveing a big fight with his horse. Cant get him down to the water. Traveled 12 miles to day.

Monday Aug the 10th 1868

Cattle done fine last night. Seminoles are lyeing around camp all morning, rather troublesome. They all want to trade but some of them have nothing to trade. I am on a trade with one. He wants to trade a buck hide for a lame yearling. Have traded. Adare told me to give it or we wouldent trade. In sight of Smiths herd. We will travel together clear through. I would like to live here if inhabited by whites. Got off of the right road this morning. Traveled east 5 ms. Now we have to go 5 ms west to get back to the road. The road runs north that we were in

12. This is the South Canadian River. Chickasaw land was south of the river, Seminole and Creek land to the north. The herd probably crossed the river a few miles southeast of modern Purcell, Oklahoma.

and I think we need a guide. Though nobody ever traveled it but Charlie.[13] I am vexed. [*page 30*] The right road is a very large road. We took off to the right on an Indian trail. Noon on a high prairie ridge. No water. More grumbling in camp today than ever. Adare says Witt led off rong. Wit says Adare did. Both rong, + boys all mad. Bosses all mad at Boys. Boys all mad at Bosses. We found the road at the old Seminole Agency.[14] Cattle ran in muddy boggy creek. Had thunder geting them out. Came North 2 ms through thick timber came to a little branch. Not much water. Cattle in it drinking. Got them out. Traveled one mile. Camp at Indian houses. No grass, no water, no nothing. [*page 31*]

Tuesday Aug 11th 1868

Cattle herded easy last night. Some Indians came to camp with corn watermelons. Bought them from them. Start at sunup. Have to go several miles to get water. Cattle made several attempts to run this morning. Got them stoped every time. Came very near runing into Smiths herd. Came to prairie. Found enough water to cook + water horses. Have breakfast here. Looks very much like rain. Cattle feeding fine. Boys deviling Bean about his

13. Bailey never provides Charlie's last name, but this entry suggests that Charlie had traveled this route earlier.

14. The Seminole Agency, also called Council Town, was located on the west bank of Agency Creek near Wanette, Pottawatomie County, Oklahoma. The Seminole capital was located there until 1866, when it was moved to Wewoka in modern Seminole County, Oklahoma.

Cistern [his canteen], which is the largest one I ever saw. Came 5 ms. Found a little water. Adare is about to sell out to the Indians for trafic such as Buck skin Beans onions and Roasting years. Passed over a good country to day + yesterday. Creek bottom especially, which (the Creeks) have [*page* 32] very red banks are about as red as a brick. Very boggy. Cross Little River near Shawnee Villiage.[15] Found plenty of water for the cattle. Banks very bad. Bottom brushy. Travel down the river about 2 miles before we could get into it. Had fun keeping the cattle out of it. Brush very thick but we kept them in the edge of a valley. Weeds as thick as they could stand and about 12 feet high. Came 3 ms. Overtook Smiths herd on a long brang [*sp?*]. Plenty of water + grass. They were nooning. We came on 5 ms found water in a branch in prairie for horses. We have traveled through timber all day, but are in a whaleing big prairie. Now has rained on us all day. We have camped in a little grove to night. Consequently have plenty wood, Adare hired an old Sha[w]nee [*page* 33] Indian to travel with him this evening. Gave him 5.00 for nothing in the world. I will remark right here that I never saw any one so taken with Indians as he + family are. He believes every thing they tell him + does most any way they say. Now his hireing the old Indian may be doubted by some but there is too much proof. His excuse was he had to have a guide this evening but

15. The herd probably crossed Little River southwest of modern Tecumseh, Oklahoma.

there is but one road + the timber was so thick that it would be hard work to drive through it out of the road. They rode in front all evening. As for the water we couldent have missed it. There was but one little hole in the branch + it was right on the road. I have just eat my supper + have come out to relieve balence of my guard while they eat. [*page 34*] Our course been north. Came 11 ms. Cattle been scared all day. Mad[e] several attempts to run. Look out to nigh. We are apt to have a run to night. Smith's herd just comeing in sight. Too dark to write More. Anon

Wednesday Aug. 12th

We had the hardest time last night imaginable. I got up at 10 oclock. Never got off of my horse no more until day light. As I predicted we had 2 of the worst kind of Stampedes. The 1st time they made a break about 9 [?] oclock. Run about ½ hour. Got them to runing around in a circle. Dont Sanders on herd with his guard + they managed to stop them. They rested [*page 35*] then until about 2 hours before day, then jewhilikens how they run. It was raining, came a loud keen clap of thunder. They turned all loose. It was so dark we couldent see them. Sometimes we were right in the midle of herd. You bet they made the ground roar. We couldent circle them. Finally got them cut into or divided. Circled part of them. Balance ran off before we found out they were separated. Such holering and runing around you never heard. Some of the boys couldent find their horses som bridles out of the way. Some couldent find blankets but all that was not afraid found every thing very readily. Women scared nearly to death. Children screaming. Some of the boys holering at the cattle when the cattle were not near them [*page 36*] but they swore they wer comeing right towards them. Dud Rogers, the spunkiest man in the crowd when there is no danger started to climb a tree + leave the women to fight it out as best they could. He was so bad scared he fell out of the tree and holered for some one to run here + help me up this tree. (Nobody went.) Finally day broke. We soon saw several head was gone. We circled, found 3 large trails. Folered them. Succeeded in finding about two hundred head but mised some more noted steers. Witt started with Gevia [*sp?*] Follered about nine or ten miles. Found another bunch. We have to leave here to day on account of water. Two oclock all hands in. We start. Found 2 stears on trail. Just after starting an old Indian brough in 25 head [*page 37*] wanted $5.00 per head. Adare gave him $5.00 for all + started. It is my opinion his old hired Indian + some others done the mischief for us last night but he dont think they would treat him in that maner. (No indeed) I feel very dull, drousy + sleepy to day. Gus + Negroe Ben had a big quarel about a blanket. Ben being a Negroe got the blanket.[16] Adare hired two Shawnee Indians to go the trip as guides when he

16. "Negro Ben" is one of two black cowboys identified by Bailey as being on the drive. The other was named Lewis. Bailey does not mention their last names.

has traveled the road several times or twice at least.[17] Before leaveing camp about 20 Negroes came up to us, US Soldiers headed by a white Negroe, a Lieutenant hunting Negroe deserters which passed us last Sunday. Seven in number the Lieut hired six Indians to go on and overtake the Negroes. Gave them $130.00. Said his men were very much fatigued. They had rode very hard all day.[18] [*page* 38] Came two miles. Came to north fork of Canadian the pretiest little stream I ever saw.[19] Runs South east. Aford any quantity of water. One mile, came to prairie overtook Smiths herd. Traveled eight miles. Camp on branch.[20] Some timber good grass. Cam to left of road. Cattle too tired to run much tonight. Boys nearly all wore out from last nights work. Passed over a rich country today. Negroe soldier here grinding Coffee. Bought mellons corn + peas from some Indians to day [...] night.

17. Bailey is questioning the need for Indian guides since John Adare claimed he had traveled the route at least twice before. Bailey's later entries also seem to question Adare's claim of knowing the route to Kansas.

18. These troops were undoubtedly Buffalo Soldiers of the 10th U.S. Cavalry (see note 2), which supposedly had the lowest desertion rate in the army even though its soldiers were often stationed in the worst country and frequently subjected to the harshest of discipline, racist officers, poor food, inadequate equipment, and poor shelter. Between July and November 1868 a company of the 10th Cavalry stationed at Fort Arbuckle was engaged in drilling, repairing buildings, and chasing cattle rustlers and bootleggers.

19. The herd probably reached the north fork of the Canadian River just southwest of modern Shawnee, Pottawatomie County, Oklahoma.

20. Their camp was probably located northwest of modern Shawnee, Oklahoma.

"Midnight Storm and Stampede," by Henry Worrall, from Joseph McCoy's 1874 classic, *Historic Sketches of the Cattle Trade.* Jack Bailey and other cowboys with him experienced similar storms and stampedes on their 1868 trail drive. Courtesy Kansas State Historical Society, Topeka.

Thursday, Aug 13th

Had a hully [*sp?* bully?] time last night. Cattle kept quiet all night. My relief was last + the boys dident wake me until about day for which I feel thankful to them for I had a good nights rest. This is a beautiful country. Good range. [*page* 39] Country broken just enough to make it pretty. It is clear this morning. We have concluded to move half mile + lay up the balence of the day. Smith will lay up too killing a beef. Done moved got a splendid place. Plenty wood water + grass. We devil Dud nearly to death about climbing the tree. Negroe soldiers camp near us. They are resting, They are so fatigued. We all sympathise

"A Stampeded Herd," by J. Andre Castaigne (*Scribner's* magazine, 1892). Courtesy Kansas State Historical Society, Topeka.

with them in a Lonn [*sp?*]. Adare sending them a lot of fresh beef. Hope that will relieve them. Some one of the Negroes said they had nothing to eat but some bacon + white fish light bread cheese rice + crakers. Said their coffee, tea, + sugar got wet as if they were spoilt. He was done eating 'til he got back to Fort. Lord God, less quit talking about them. You bet Charlie + old lady spreads themselves before the <u>Gentlemanly</u>, <u>Lieut.</u> [*page 40*] We are in the creek Country. The north fork of Canadian separates the Creeks + Shawnee's. Well sun is siting. Been a beautiful day, but a very lonesome one for me. I have been out on herd all day writeing + thinking of my little family, do hope they are well and doing, well. Boy

"In Camp, the Texas Cattle Trade," by Frenzeny and Tavernier (*Harper's Weekly*, May 2, 1874). Courtesy Kansas State Historical Society, Topeka.

have got the cattle nearly rounded for the night. Cattle been no trouble to day. Got plenty water + grass.

Friday Aug 14th

No trouble last night with cattle. I am relieveing a guard. Breakfast is prepareing. Trying to get an early start. Boys all rested up + lively. Some of them slept all day yesterday. Bean is unwell this morning. He has several bad boils on his set down. Is not able to drive to day. Pass two

Creeks this morning, plenty of [*page 41*] water, which make three Creeks in 5 ms. travel all got lots of water, all in prairie good camping, ground + + +. Stop to noon in a little grove. Branch on the right of road, a beautiful round hole of clear water in head of branch. Here we meet Crawford and one of the Kutch boys going home. Dident have but few minutes to talk with them. I write back home by them.[21] Came 3 miles. Find a pretty clear creek. Banks boggy + steep. A good place to water cattle. Came out one mile. Stoped to camp in a brushy little prairie. Plenty wood + water. Struck camp in a gap between the hill and creek. The worst place we could pick to camp in. Half mile back we had the best kind of a prairie but an old lieing Indian to[ld] Charlie that there was a good place on a head, so he struck out. Cuss the Indians. I wish they would stay away. We camp in a very brushy place, + the prairie to herd in is very small, good night. [*page 42*]

Saturday Aug the 15th

All right this morning. Fixing to start herding. Ground bad last night. If we had stoped a piece back to right of road we could have done some better, Smith in sight. Left camp traveled up the creek in a pretty level valley. Good

21. Crawford may be Simpson Crawford, a well-known stock raiser from Palo Pinto County, Texas, who apparently had sold a cattle herd in Abilene. The Kutch boy probably was a son of W. C. Kutch, a native of Kentucky, who moved to Jack County, Texas, in 1855. He fathered thirteen children by his first wife and seven children by his second wife. Bailey apparently sent with them a letter to his wife in Parker County, Texas.

grass plenty water but unhandy. Road runs ½ between the creek + a branch about 150 yards apart. If we had come 1/4 m futher we would have had a bully Place to herd + camp in. But didint know it. Leave the valley go up hill on a pretty post oak ridge. Travel 5 ms came to Creek. Plenty water. We are on the Gano Trail.[22] crossed the creek stoped to noon on bank. Indians comeing with the Negroe Deserters. The Indian Adare hired for guide is at camp. He went with the other Indians to catch the Negroes. [*page 43*] Bean suffering very much with his boils are too bad to ride. Frank Martin is driveing for him.[23] Frank + Ben (Negroe) like to run together. Today wish they had. If I had been present I would have made Frank mall him. Bosses all in bad humor today. Old lady high cock of the walk. Right diverting the talk around camp is all about guarding none satisfied. They make last night out 19 ½ hours long. Have no watch. Some swears they stood over 2 hours. Our general course to day north but our trail runs various ways. I am siting in shade of a post oak. Can see waggons on the creek. Cattle

22. The Gano Trail was used during the Civil War by Gano's Texas Cavalry Battalion, named for Confederate Brig. Gen. Richard Montgomery Gano. After seeing service in Kentucky and Tennessee, the unit was sent to Indian Territory where it served under Gen. Samuel Bell Maxey, who had six thousand Indians in his command.

23. Frank Martin probably was the son of Thomas Martin, a native of South Carolina, who moved first to Missouri and then in the 1850s to Parker County, Texas. The 1860 U.S. census rolls for Parker County record Thomas Martin's occupation as farmer and list several children, including a Frank Martin, who would have been twenty-two in 1868.

feeding in valley. I am on a high hill. Prairie sets in here. Has appearance of a very large one. Passed over a good valley to day. Timber very heavy for this country, hickory post oak [*page 44*] elm cottonwood + walnut. Still in the Creek Nation. No Settlement. Say we will not see any more til we get to deep fork of Canadian. Leve camp at 3 oclock. Traveled three miles turned turn to right of road found water in head of ravine 300 yds from road. Take up for the night. Course north. Cam 9 ms.

Sunday August the 16th

Had a good place to camp last night. Cattle done fine. Plenty grass + water. Came up a rain while last relief was out. Turned the cattle from the wind and let them go. Found all of them easy this morning. None of them out of sight. Mrs Martins baby fell out of the wagon. Dident hurt it. I throwed featherkill down this morning. Backed out the camp on a fair rassel [*sp?*]. Get an early start. [*page 45*] Came 4ms to a creek plenty water. Very brushy bottom. Came out ½ mile in the bottom. Came to a singular looking lake 300 yds long 20 wide six or eight feet deep. Met 3 men here with pack horse going to Texas. Very hungry. Gave them something to eat, rolled out. They tell of a left hand trail 7 m a head. Advise us to take it. They say it is clear of brush + is nearest plenty watter + +. Cross another creek. Water red but a good place to water cattle. Came out three miles to a small prairie. We in one end, Smith in other. Stoped to noon. Smith killed a beef send us one quarter. Annie sick to

"The Texas Cattle Trade, Guarding the Herd" (*Harper's Weekly*, 1874). Courtesy Colorado Historical Society, Denver.

day. Passed lots of water to day caused by heavy rain last night. Start two oclock. Travel north. Come to deep fork of the Canadian.[24] Tis a large creek rock bottom. Had considerable trouble crossing. Got out to prairie dark came 11 ms to day. [*page 46*]

Monday Aug the 17th 1868

Appearance of rain all night. Cattle done very well. Ben + Wit had a rowe just before day. Ben wouldent get up. Wit struck him with quirt. Ben swore he would quit

24. The "deep fork of the Canadian" is more likely the Deep Fork River. The herd probably crossed the river northeast of modern Luther in far northeast Oklahoma County, Oklahoma.

when day come. And when day come he rolled out. Adare followed him. He said to give him Something for his labor but I see Ben comeing back with him. I dont know what he is going to do. No settlements near + the Negroe afoot will starve to death before he could get any where but I say let him ris. Well he has got to camp, Glory. Waiting for Smith to come up. We are at forks of trail. Sun is comeing out. Hope no rain to day. The right hand road is very brushy + much the fartherest rout but still Adare is on a quandary which to take. Why I cant tell, the other is all prairie. [*page 47*] Plenty water. Good range + wood enough for camping purposes. Took left hand. Came to a good spring in head of ravine. Stoped to noon. Good grove to shade in. Plenty water in holes and looks like lasting at this time runing but caused by recent hard rains. Course west of north today. Our Indian guides left us this morning. Glad of it. Annie is some better to day. Start 3 oclock. Kept on our course. Came about 5 miles. Camp on a branch ½ mi from road. Travel down branch nearly one mile before we find water. Where we left the road is a splendid spring in the brush one hundred yds to left of road. Leave it for Smith. He is behind yet.

Tuesday Aug the 18th 1868

Had the devil last night in shape of a storm which lays over any thing of the kind I ever witnessed. The wind came in whirls down this hollow, tremendous [*page 48*] rain. Keen loud claps of thunder and the most vivid, forked, scariest pretiest + fastest lightning I ever saw. It came up while the first relief was out which was mine. We turned the cattle towards a point of timber and went to camp, in a hurry too. Just did get in, in time. It came with a vengeance. Clouds came every way. Met over us, and such a clash. I thought once or twice we were done for. Some of the boys badly scared. Our tent blew down. The old lady holered for help to hold her tent down. We let ours rip and every fellow for himself. Some went to wagons. Some to other tent. Everything soaking wet. Finally abated. Children got to crying. Women scolding. Some of the boys singing and all talking about the storm. Not much sleeping going on. All cold wet + mad. Well, but takeing every [*page 49*] thing in consideration all passed off very well. Our cattle scatered very little this morning. Smiths herd is all over the country. From all appearances he had a big stamped. A great many of his in our herd. We rounded ours in before breakfast. I dont think we have lost one. Stay here to day. Ground too soft to travel, + Smith cant leave on account of lost cattle. I have been out in rain nearly all day. Close for the night. Had to all herd to day.

Tuesday, Aug 18th 1868

I have dated this rong, please turn over. Wronge.

[*page 50*] *Wednesday Aug 19th*

No trouble last night. Some wild bulls got in the herd. Had several big fights but dident disturb the cattle. It cleared off last night and we had a very heavy dew, almost equal to a rain. The Indians sent word to day that they had stoped some cattle. Smiths I suppose. Shure enough his cattle had a big run the stormy night + he has lost several. Leave here to day. Dont Sanders + I went back with Smith + one of his hands after the cattle the Indians had. We went back ten miles found 25 head of Beef stears with the Indians. As we came back found 25 head more, which is about all he has missing. Got back late in the evening. Had moved about 5 ms to a branch to left of road. Water in head of branch, for horses + cooking purposes + + +

[*page 51*] *Thursday Aug the 20th*

Cattle done fine last night. Fixing to start in a very large prairie. Good grass but I dont think there is much lasting water in this country. No settlements. Still in Creek Nation. This side where we camp is a splendid everlasting spring one hundred yards to the right of the road. Runs from under a large flat rock under a large tree. Our course now is north east. Came 5 ms. Came to a creek. Not much water in it but ½ mile this side of the creek is a spring branch which affords any amt of water. The spring is 20 ydds from the road to the right here. We are nooning. Start 2 oclock. Came 4 ms. Found plenty water in head of ravine. A good place to camp. Traveled over a long ridge. In Sight of Salt fork of Arksas River.[25]

25. Probably the Cimarron River and in the vicinity of modern Perkins in Payne County, Oklahoma. Bailey had not yet reached the Salt Fork of the

Traveled North 10 ms. Killed a beef. Eat drink + be merry. Wind up for the night.

[*page* 52] *Friday Aug the 21st*

Pulled up camp 8 oclock. Traveled 2 + ½ miles. Came to the river. Sounding to see if fordable for wagons. Across swam ponies + cattle. The largest horses waded. Proped up waggon beds. Smith crossed right behind us with little trouble. Travel over a beautiful hickory ridge. Land very rich. 5 ms came to prairie. Struck camp on branch lots of water. I believe it is the best country I ever saw. Smith in sight at grove. Had no dinner to day.

Saturday Aug 22n 1868

Cattle all right this morning. Pull up camp. Get early start. Smiths oxen gone. Found them. I see them comeing with them. Two tall round mountains [hills] off to right of road about eight miles from trail. Found plenty [*page* 53] so far to day but the most of it is caused by recent rains. Came 8 miles. Nooned at a spring 200 yds to left of road under a black Jack. Some of the boys killed a wild stear to day. Brought part in. This country has a great many wild cattle in it mostly bulls. Crosed 2 large creeks tributarys of Salt fork. I am not well to day. Have a pain in my side, got Frank Martin to drive in my place. I am riding in waggon. Country very level. Little groves

---

Arkansas River, a stream that flows west to east in north-central Oklahoma and into the Arkansas River near present-day Ponca City, Oklahoma.

scatered over the country. Came 4 miles. Camp on creek. Plenty wood water + grass. Good place to herd on the other side of creek. Course east of north. Smith in sight. Came 15 miles today. Now for supper.

Sunday Aug the 23d 1868

Another Sunday, almost sick this morning. Got here in the night last night, every one in bad humor, still mad [*page 54*] tis noon. Passed two creeks this morning left road ¼ mile to the right, passed a good camping place ½ [?] Mile back on road. Start course north, traveled over a larg ridge 4 miles. Came to creek plenty timber on it. Been rideing with Dud all day. Cant tell which is the worst his continual gab or my side. Adare thinks we are on the Sarquasqence river but not certain.[26] It is a very rocky bad place to cross but shallow bottom very brushy but narrow banks show to be muddy in bad weather. Had to work on the bank of three creeks. Sick. All convalescent this evening. Camp in creek. Course north. Distance 8 miles. Crawl in for the night.

Monday Aug the 24th

Pulled up camp 8 oclock. Sick. All better this morning caught a lame stear + took neck yoke off of him. Water 2 miles spring in head of [*page 55*] branch to left of trail under a large elm. Start 3 oclock. Cross 2 branches. Plenty

26. The "Sarquasqence River" has not been identified, though Bailey frequently spelled words by how they sounded. It may have been an Indian name for the Salt Fork of the Arkansas River.

water in both. Came 8 miles today. Course north. Something going to hapen for we have got a good camping place. Lots of water wood + grass. Camp to right of trail 200 yds, water in ravine. Bud gave Ben a good curseing + would have whiped him if he had not humbled down. Ben has been in habit of sliping off from herd + going to camp + they would laugh at him for it. Bud mad[e]. Him roll out for the herd. Wish he would have mauled him good. All rounding. In for the night.

Tuesday, Aug 25th 1868

All passed off night last night. We came unexpectlaly on the Arkansas River this morning.[27] Such rejoiceing I never saw over a little thing. We were all badly fooled. Adare says now [*page* 56] he knew it couldent be far but was thinking we would be til 12 reach it. But last night got mad because Dont Sanders + Witt wouldent agree it was 60 miles to it. Said he knew by a tall mountain that you can see in the forks of river. I am satisfyed we are 50 miles or more from the crossing. He crossed it before. River is very wide but shallow. Only a few places that swim the calves. I gues it is ½ mile wide or more the way we have to cross. A great deal quick sand. Got across with little trouble. Came out ½ miles. Rise high mountain on

27. Bailey may have crossed the Salt Fork of the Arkansas River near where it flows into the Arkansas River south of modern Ponca City, Oklahoma. East of that point the Arkansas River curves back and forth, which would have required more than one crossing, but Bailey makes reference to only one crossing.

Texas cattle watering on a trail drive. The illustration, by an unidentified artist, appeared on an advertising trade card published in the late nineteenth century by the St. Louis Beef Canning Company. Courtesy David Dary.

a very pretty level prairie. Cam 2 + ½ miles. Strike camp to right of road. Find plenty water in head of ravine. Good wood. Splendid grass. Cam 3 miles today. Cant tell yet how far to white settlements. Had no dinner. Some of the boys got ducked while [*page* 57] crossing river caused by horses falling down. Les go to supper. Here goes says Bud.

Wednesday Aug the 26 th /68

Some appearance of rain this morning. Clowdy + very warm. Smith is in sight. He crossed the river esay. I am on guard this morning, while breakfast is prepareing. This is a good pretty country. You can see tall round peaks in every direction. When we first started it was all jokes but now every one trys to see who can beat grumbling. All knact [*sp?*] To old lady quarreling. Geting to have a right sulky crowd. Start 8 oclock. Came two miles. Came to a large trail leading west. Supose it is Osages going out on a hunt. We are in their country. Cam 7 ms. Stoped to noon on branch 200 yds to right of road. Noon 3 hours. Start off all right. Joe Martin lost his whip to day. I lost Featherkiles knife, mine too. [*page* 58] Not my day to herd. Came 12 ms to day. Stoped to camp on a large creek. Adare says it is Walnut. Sanders says Walnut is 50 miles ahead yet. I am siting on a large flat rock. Find siveral names carved on it. I put mine down too. Find a note on a tree adviseing drovers to go to right of the creek + we will cut off 10 miles.[28] Adare says it is a lie. I dont know. By traveling nearly all day find out the note was right in the evening. Came nearly back to where we camped last night tis not over two miles. I start for camp, here goes for a hearty supper.

Thursday Aug 27

Dud flew off at the handle last night + moved his cooking to himself. Cant blame him much. Poor fellow pecked to death. Fixing for an early start. Adare gave up that he is mistaken about the creek. Tis not walnut. [*page* 59] Left the ridge road. Came down mountain into a very large valley. Pass a tall hill with rocks piled up on it.

28. The note found on a tree advising cattle drovers to take a certain path suggests that many trail herds were following this same route in 1868, which was far to the east of what became the Chisholm Trail.

Suppose it is for a guide. Noon under a little blackjack grove. Grass fresh (late burn) + good. 3 ms. Came to a creek in prairie. Plenty water. No wood hardly. Killing a beef. Came 9 ms to day.

Friday Aug the 28th

Cattle herded easy last night. Had a gay old time roasting beef. Frank stood my guard. While the boys were eating supper last night Mrs. Adare called Negroe Lewis + invited him to eat supper at her table. He accepted, + it made some of the boys mad of course. I was on herd with Bud. The boys swore they would quit next morning if it was not explained + to cap it all, while we were eating breakfast this morning [*page 60*] she sent Ben (Negroe) over a plate of milk gravy which was quite a luxury to any of us. Bud + I talked to them about it. They tryed to fix it up. We patched it over so the boys were a little satisfyed but dident like. Lewis was in all their private consultations. But I did not like such political differences myself but I knew how it was before.[29] All right. I rec[k]on. Came three miles. Came down a mountain, into a beautiful valley passed between two large round mounds. Neither over one hundred yds from road. Bud killed a prairie hen. Cross a large creek. Plenty water. Like

29. "Before" undoubtedly refers to life in Texas before the Civil War. For nine years following the Civil War, Texas was in turmoil. Texans attempted to solve political, social, and economic problems produced by the war. Emancipation changed the labor system, and the end of slavery saw race relations severely strained.

to a had stampede while crossing. Noon on right of road. 'Tis a beautiful large + level valley. Start 2 oclock. Came ½ mile to one of the prettiest little creeks I ever saw. Not a bit [*page 61*] of timber on it. Very clear, large deep holes. Boys all swam their horses + swam around awhile themselves 'til all tired. Start. Cross another Osage trail to day leading west. Very large. Looks like it has been traveled years. Travel up the creek in a pretty valley all evening. Camp near creek to right of road on ravine. Sanders found a cow + calf on the prairie droped by some drover ahead. Course to day north. Round up for th night.

Saturday August 28th 1868

Rained last night. Turned the cattle loose. Found them all this morning. Very handy. Eat Breakfast. Early ready to start. Witt + Smith roll out this morning to hunt the settlement. Diferent opinions as to the distance we have traveled up the creek all day. Had several hard showers on us. We are all wet cold + mad. + nearly [*page 62*] out of provision. Prospect of a rainy night. Came north, 6 miles

Sunday Aug the 30th 1868

Another Sabbath. Hope all right at home. If they are doing well it is more than we can say. Cloudy and very dark all night. Cattle a great deal of trouble. One of the coldest dampest + foggiest mornings imaginable. A severe norther up. Witt + Smith not returned yet. Martin + Mrs

A had the bigest quarel I ever heard. Old lady beat him easy. John Cause, left camp.[30] Quit the creek. At last came up a mountain. Can see over a large scope of level prairie country. Can see two large round mounds off to our right. Suppose they are twenty miles distant. 5 ms. Nooning on branch. While there a dark angry looking cloud came up. [*page 63*] Heavy thunder keen lightning and such a rain. Slack up. We started. Traveled only one mile. Came another severe cloud and turned the whole heavens loose. As it were had to take up wind hard + cold from the north. Blew the rain in our faces + the cattle. As horses wont face it so we struck camp. All chilled nearly through. Just as we stoped rain came harder. Wind harder. All nearly froze. Hard work to kindle fire. Everything so thouroughly soaked with water. Plenty wood but unhandy. But we finally got a large supply of green hickory + ash wood. Built a large log heap between the two tents as close as we could without burning and - and- and- Bunked for the night. Let the cattle rip. I wouldent herd to night for the herd. So her [*erased words*]

[*page 64*] *Monday, Aug 31st 1868*

Dident do so well last night. All wet but kept in a good humor. Bean got a little ashy because he couldent get supper. Bud + I managed to keep some of our blankets dry. Some of the boys lay all night rolled up in a wet

30. "John Cause" may be Bailey's shorthand way of saying that John Adare left camp because his wife was having a quarrel with someone else.

blanket. Rained bigest part of the night. After we lay down found Beans Wallet of clothes. He had a pair of right new Soldier pants which were dry. The temptation was too great so I hooked them out hauled of my wet clothes crauled in them and I slep - high + dry. Bean mised them and hunted about ½ hour. Couldent find them. So next morning I sliped them back. I never saw a fellow hunt like hed did. Finely I told him he had overlooked them. Perhaps they were in the wallet, bet me a treat they were not. Looked + shure enough they [*page* 65] were there. He said he couldent see into it. Finally some of the boys told him the joke. He laughed it off very well. Said as he dident loose them. He was satisfyed. Well the supposition of Adare is that we are on little Walnut but tis mine that we are not in 40 miles of it. Boys not returned from settlements yet. Had to boil over the old grouns of coffee this morning. Ground is very muddy + boggy. 3 miles. Cross another large creek. Road runs between creek + mountain. Cam down mountain in a large valley to another large creek. I + Adare drove in a left stear + lame cow. Noon on crossing banks very steep + difficult to cross. Conclud to rest balence of day. Cattle wont feed. Want to ramble. Trying to water them. Banks steep and slipery. Rounding up for the night.

[*page* 66] *Tuesday September 1st*

Killed a poor yearling yesterday. Meanest beef I ever saw. Wel all told Charlie we couldent eat it. But Lewis said it was fat + that decided the thing. It was a little grass guted thing. Had to throw most of it away. Cattle herded easy last night. We hobbled one cow that left her calf. I never so as much belly ache as was in camp last night. All very hungry + tired. Had no salt to put on our little yearling. Broiled it. The more we cooked it the biger it got. Eat it half done + the consequence was all had the trots all night. Had a big laugh at camp next morning. All passes of[f] with no serious results Cross another Osage trail this morning. Witt + Smith not returned yet. Travel over a hilly country this morning a few miles. 10 oclock [*page 67; portion of page is missing, torn out*] meet the provisions. Witt [...] returned. Bring plenty prov [...] a hack to drive out with [...] got lots coffee. They [...] saw Eahart, Et, A [...]15 ms ahead of u [...] is Stoped to n [...] lively, old n [...] seeing ho [...] without [...] folks live, con [...] to eat drink + be m [...] returned from Smiths [...] ed me to a team of good old [...] it was a treat too.[31] Rounding up for to night. Passed very little water to day, but the branch we are on affords plenty watter for a large herd or any amt of stock. Course to day north came 9 miles.

[*page 68; portion of page is torn out*] [...] *dnesday September 2nd*

[...] Third guard stood nearly [...] Bud + I came very near [...] slighted, it wa daylight [...] us up, we wont get

31. Both pages 67 and 68 have words missing because they are the front and back of a sheet in the journal that is partially torn out.

[...] are on guard now [...] eing had Company [...] t John and [...] him out [...] that is [...] Ellow believes it [...] poilt it all makeing [...] fellow for believeing it [...] ered him so he had to run [...] from him then the old lady picked him up + rattle rattle rattle. I cant write. Boys all evedroping her. They swear that she has more cattle than you can put in any one county in Texas. She says he is one of the finest young men she ever saw, says he does more work in one month than [*page 69*] a Texas boy will do in a year. I dident think it would make her mad to ask her what he done with all his money + that he aint smart + so on but you bet it wont do to talk about him. He is down on Rebs + that suits fine. If some of us could get him out we would sell him so quick he wont know what to do well. He is the Yankee chap tha the boys hired to drive them out in his hack. The Creek we thought Walnut (or the one Adare said) is Goose Creek.[32] So say pearty. Came seven miles to a large road leading East too Gibson West to Abbaline where we strike the road is a tolerable large creek.[33] Plenty water wood + grass. Came 3 miles to creek. Stoped to camp. Meet one of Sheltons hands on his way to Texas. This is a very good range country but is not as good as Jack Montague Wise palapinto or part of Parker Counties [*page 70*] but our cattle + horses are doing well as could be expected. They are not falling off any yet. I change with Martin

32. Perhaps modern Chilocco Creek, which runs east to west just south of the Kansas border in Indian Territory. It flows into the Arkansas River.

33. "Abbaline" is Abilene, Kansas.

awhile this morning. He on my horse I in his wagon. Bud + his horse is haveing a hard fight. Came 10 ms. Stope for the night.

Thursday, September 3d 1868

On creek on right of road 200 yds. Came up a tight little norther last night in fore part of night, when I started out on guard. I left my coat at camp. Dud came out to stand my place out. I started to cam very warm went strait to camp. By the time I got my bed fixed + in it was cold enough to have two blanket for cover. Still very cold this morning. Smith close to us talks of going on this morning to look him out a place to rest up awhile before driveing into market. Adare went ahead [*page 71*] yesterday to look out a place to stop. Has not returned yet. We are in 4 miles of Earharts camp. Waiting now for Adare to return. Boys scuffling in camp. Joe wollering. Dud, Adare returned. Liff Earhart with him.[34] We move three or four miles to rock creek not far from where it runs in walnut about one mile above the road. Meet Joe

34. Liff Earhart may have been a son of Joseph B. Earhart, who managed a stage station on the Butterfield Overland Mail at Hog Eye sixteen miles east of Jacksboro, Jack County, Texas. When the stage line shifted to a northern route during the Civil War, Earhart lost his job. By then, however, he had built a prosperous cattle ranch in Jack County. Bailey's journal suggests the Earharts were also trailing a herd of longhorns north and were close by. Later entries, including one on September 7, mention Joe Earhart (Joseph B. Earhart?). It is not known if this is the same Joseph B. Earhart who was earlier associated with Colbert's Ferry on the Red River (see note 98). At this point Bailey was apparently unaware that he and the others on the trail drive had crossed into Kansas.

Henry Martin.[35] Found a good camping place. Good spring, plenty timber on creek. Lots of water in creek. Kill a beef fat baron cow. I believe I had a light chill today. Night.

Friday, September 4th 1868 AD

I was sick all night. Dident stand guard. Cattle all right this morning. Only three on herd today. Balence building corelle [corral] in bend of creek. By night they will have 40 acres fenced in, only one string of fence to make. Be sufficient to hold the cattle. [*page* 72] Range is not as good here as is represented. Good enough for summer but not one sprig of winter grass. We are near the settlements. One or two miles above us a man named McCabe is living.[36] Has small stock about four miles. There are several houses on Walnut. Got the pen done so we are done guarding of a night herd out all day pen of a night. Our cattle have fallen off very little if any. We shall stay here several weeks as we cant drive in to the settlements until December.[37] I will from this on only

35. Probably Joseph H. Martin, stock raiser, whose name appears in the 1860 U.S. census rolls for Wise County, Texas. Martin, a native of Kentucky, would have been forty years old in 1868 and three years older than Bailey.

36. Probably D. L. McCabe, one of the first settlers in Rock Creek Township, located in what is now northern Cowley County, Kansas, a county that borders on Oklahoma. Rock Creek Township is just south of the Butler County line in Kansas. There McCabe and his family had established their home west of the Walnut River. Rock Creek Township was organized in July 1868, less than three months before Bailey arrived in the area.

37. The decision to hold the herd where it was and not drive it to the settlements until December probably means that Adare and the cowboys were

mention little incidents that transpire a round camp. If I had paper I could write down several thing that I shall have to omit on that account. We have traveled 38 days, had plenty to eat and well served up only a few little quarels considering, we have got along smoothly. We cant tell yet [*page* 73] how long we shall have to stay here. Several of the beef stears are lame also some of the cows also. Well night is on us boys done pen. All rejoicing that they wont have to guard to night. Our general cours the trip has been north. Land up here is nothing like as good as I expected. McCabe say corn hits here about evry third season. This year is a total failure. Timber is very scarce. I dont think that the country will afford building timber as for fenceing. They say they dont need much as there is no loose stock to interfere with crops. The day has passed off quietly out here but I wont vouch for it in camp. I must drive in. (So loose cows).

[*page 74*] *Saturday Sept 5th 1868*

Pened in the new pen last night. Had to guard it to keep the cattle from breaking out. There is so much

---

aware of the law passed by the Kansas legislature and signed by the governor early in 1867. It prohibited the driving of cattle from Texas or Indian Territory between March and December except west of the Sixth Meridian and south of a line running from northeast of modern McPherson, Kansas, to the Colorado border. Their herd was already east of the Sixth Meridian. Accounts of Texas cowboys building fences to hold their cattle on a trail drive are uncommon. Texas cattle herds were usually held in an area and allowed to graze while being watched by cowboys.

brush in it they dont like it. I am not well by a jug full this morning. Joe Henry Martin is here this morning. Horses took a stampede last night in the valley. Dont know what scared them. Dident run much. Been several to see us this morning. Another drove of beef passed today. Dont know where it is. Some of the boys gone out to see. Ann + Mary Hendley are gone fishing, a great many fish in the creek. Martin caught a fine mix yesterday. The say Walnut Creek is a long ways ahead of this in land timber + water. Water is not fit for use on this creek.[38] Valleys very small, up land rocky, and by [*page* 75] the by tis a poor country. I cant see why it is any better or near as good as Jack County Texas, the range is nothing to compare. Timber scarcer. Land only in valleys as good water has a green scum all over it. The spring we are at is good water. No musquit grass of consequence. They say that cattle does very well here by feeding half the year. Cattle that wintered here last winter is in good order but no fatter than cattle were on the frontier when we left. Cattle here are crossed with Durham which gives them a good appearance. But McCabe says a great many cattle die here through the 1st winter whether you feed them or not going through acclimateing. We have some cattle that looks as well as his.

38. Possibly Rock Creek, which flows northeast to southwest and into Walnut River from the east. Walnut Creek is Walnut River, which begins in northern Butler County, Kansas, and flows south into the Arkansas River at modern Arkansas City, Kansas.

[page 76] Sunday September 6th 1868

Cattle done fine last night. Dident have to guard. I had another fever yesterday. Felt sick all night. Nothing hapened to day. Part of the boys been out on herd all day. Balence lyeing around camp. They are driveing in. Mised my fever to day. All at camp.

Monday September 7th 1868

Cattle all right this morning. Mrs. Adare had fever all day yesterday. Still has some this morning. I am over mine. Several of the boys complaining to day though none of them down. Joe Earhart over to see us to day. Brings very flatering news from the R Road concerning sales of stock.[39] Martin is makeing arangements to leave us tomorrow. [*page* 77] He talks of working for McCabe. Part of Smiths hands are at camp to see us. The cattle are very hard to herd today. Brandon from Wise Co. Lex is here.[40] He is camping on Walnut Creek with cattle + horses. Sold out on condition. Has lost 40 head of his horse, and about 150 head of cattle. All beef stears. Came very near a rowe in camp today. All that kept it down was

39. Joe Earhart undoubtedly had learned details about selling cattle in Abilene and seeing them shipped east over the Union Pacific Railroad, Eastern Division.

40. Brandon from Wise County may be A. B. Brandon, who is listed along with his wife Mary in the 1860 U.S. census for Wise County, Texas. His occupation was farmer. His first name could have been Alexander. If so, Lex could be his nickname. Brandon apparently stopped to camp with Bailey and other cowboys after selling his herd. He was probably returning to Texas.

want of grit on both sides. Between Wit + Frank Martin. Frank told him he was a liar and could whip him fisticator. Witt dident want to fight that way. Threatened to shoot him but couldent get a six shooter. Nobody wouldent hold either of them. They fell out about a little settlement. Both in the rong. Nobody hurt or scared bad, Ann beged Witt not to hurt him or I suppose he would have whiped him. [*page* 78] I dont see what else kept him from it. Driveing up cattle for the night.

Tuesday September the 8th

I am out on herd this morning. Dont expect to be out all day. Dark clouds are riseing from the north west. It will rain. I am only herding 'til the guard gets breakfast. I see Brandon and Travis comeing. Cattle done well last night. All that are on the puny list are better this morning. Martin roled out this evening. I + Bud went down to Earharts camp to day. Saw McCabe boys fine cattle. They are the worst over-rated little bunch of cattle I ever saw. I dont see that they are any better than Jack County or any other musquit cattle. They are short low bunchy cattle [*page* 79] fed half the time. Horns very short, though they are good for such a country as Kansas. No more this evening.

Wednesday, September 9th

Adare starts to fall Fall River this morning to let out some of his stock on Shares this winter.[41] Witt is fixing to

41. Fall River flows from the northwest part of Greenwood County, Kansas, the county just east of Butler County, where El Dorado, Kansas, is located. The

go for flour + other provisions. Had two pony races today. Gus + Bud ran them both. Bud won both. Dud lost Guses knife (so he says). Had cush for Dinner to day. Been raining to day. This is a wet country at this time though it shows to be very drouthey. Some of the people that live here say it is not subject to drouth. Others say it is. One man says he has lived her 8 years + it has been seasonable one year in the time

[*page 80*] *Thursday Sept 10th 1868*

A heavy fog this morning. Breakfast late. Mrs Adare is at the creek washing. I have just finished her a batling [bathing?] stick. Bud Ham is shoeing his horse. Witt nor the old man have got back yet. Two men have just left here. Came to see Adare, to get some cattle to feed on Shares. Dident get any. I went down to Earharts camp this morning. Found all well + enjoying themselves finely. Evening. Witt just returned got flour, coffee and bacon. Rounding up for the night.

Friday September 11th 1868

All up this morning. Boys gone out to kill a beef. A man here enquireing for Cumbey's Camp.[42] Two men here for cattle to keep on shares. I gues they will get some.

---

town of Fall River in Greenwood County was not founded until 1879, but in 1868 an early settler named J. D. Allen was engaged in cattle raising along Fall River. It is likely that Adare arranged to leave some of his cattle with Allen on shares.

42. A man asking about the location of Cumbey's camp suggests that there may have been another trail herd owned by Edward Cumby, a farmer near the

Texas cattle fording the Arkansas River near the new settlement of Wichita, Kansas, in July 1869. The town was surveyed one year earlier, about the time the cattle herd driven by Jack Bailey and others reached a point some twenty miles southeast of where this photograph was taken. Wichita became a cattle town after the railroad arrived in the spring of 1871. Courtesy Ignace Mead Jones Collection of James R. Mead Papers, Wichita State University Libraries, Dept. of Special Collections.

They only want 60 head to feed this winter. [*page 81*] Gus bough a fine saddle from one of them. I think he made a good trade. Witt bought a fancy bridle from the same man that Gus got the saddle. These Kansas fellows

town of Decauter in Wise County, Texas. Cumby, a native of Virginia, is listed in the 1860 U.S. census for Wise County along with his son William, who in 1868 would have been eighteen. His father would have been fifty.

would sell their clothes off their back for a yearling. I never saw men want stock as bad in my life. This has been a very lively day in camp. Men will stay with us tonight.

Saturday September 12th 1868

Our Company left this morning. One of them left his six shooter. Had rain last night. Wind blew very hard but that is nothing uncommon here. Wind blows very hard all the time. It has cleared off this morning. Bids fair to be a very pretty day. Evening. Mrs Adare Annie + myself went visiting to day. Went to McCabes. Had a very pleasant visit of it considering. The girls showed all the clothes they had. Dident [*page* 82] take long either. Old lady [Mrs. McCabe] spouted mightly but Mrs Adare had more finery than they ever saw, so she says.

Sunday Sept 15th 1868

I was not well last night. I had a very severe pain in my side. A norther came up sometime in the night wind blew hard + cold. Had a general singing in camp last night. Every boy singing at the same time and all carrying his own tune. Gus sung us some Bean Creek songs. Bean sung the Beaver Cap.[43] Gus sung so solemn we got

43. "Bean Creek songs" may be ballads that were sung back in Texas. The words to the "Beaver Cap" song are as follows:

I'll sing a little song—
It won't take me very long—
About my life concerning,
About the beaver cap I wore
Before my locks were turning.

Chorus: Oh, sing true, fa la, sing wax,
Fa la, sing true a la la lay.

I went to town that very day
To buy me a hat, sir.
The very first thing they showed to me
Was a broad-brimmed beaver cap, sir.
(*Chorus*)
I bought that hat; I took it home,
And placed it on my bed, sir,
And every time that I woke up,
I set it on my head, sir.
(*Chorus*)
I went to work the very next day,
A-feeling very sad, sir.
When I got home, my mother had a hen
Set in my beaver cap, sir.
(*Chorus*)
I picked them eggs up one by one;
I guess I had some fun, sir.
I tossed them at my mother's back;
I hit her as she run, sir.
(*Chorus*)
My daddy come home that very night;
You bet he made me hop, sir.
He raised big blisters on my back
With my old beaver cap, sir.
(*Chorus*)
He beat me and banged me; he swore he would hang me.
He troubled me out of my life, sir,
And all the remedy I could find
Was to marry me a wife, sir.
(*Chorus*)
I . . . them gals; I hugged them gals,
And . . . them on my lap, sir.
They's all the time a-picking the fur
Of my old beaver cap, sir.
(*Chorus*)
I married me a wife; she was a dove,
The jolly of my life, sir,

to groaning for him. Dud sung some very good songs, + by the by.[44] He is a good singer. He also sung several comic songs which were good. It was midnight when we went to sleep. Old Lady dident like it a bit. She holered at us several time but the more she holered the louder we sung. There is three men here to day [*page* 83] after cattle. I dont think they like the prospect. Adare not here.

Monday September 14th

All up this morning. Liff Earhart spent the night with us last night. The men that were here yesterday are still here. Been cuting out cattle all day for the 2 men that came first. In now for diner. Have cut out 100 head of mother cows for him. They are to keep them three years on shares. Two more waiting to get some on same terms. Wont cut theirs out til tomorrow. Got the cattle pened for the night. Gus recieved his fine saddle to day. This is my birth day, wish I had a cake.

Until one day, she abused
My old beaver cap, sir.
(*Chorus*)
She raised a row that very day,
And took me by the nap, sir.
Tossed me out into the yard,
And stomped my beaver cap, sir.

See Vance Randolph, *Ozark Folksongs*, 4 vols. (Columbia: State Historical Society of Missouri, 1946–50). The lyrics for "Beaver Cap" may be found in volume 3 (1949), entry no. 355.

44. Because of Bailey's reference to songs, it was first believed he was referring to the old song "Bye and Bye." Bailey, however, uses the expression "by the by" (meaning "by the way") in an earlier entry on Saturday, September 5, and again in an entry on Monday, September 27.

Tuesday..Sept..15th 1868

Had a hard storm last night. Water run under our camp. Got everthing perfectly wet + muddy. We all had to stand up balence of the night..had six men [*page 84*] in our tent besides our own layout so we were crow[d]ed to the gunels. We did intend starting for Abbaline this morning but the gound is too soft and muddy and it is still raining but not hard. 12 oclock. Still misting rain. Several of us went grape hunting to day. Found lots of grapes + hackberrys. Looks like raining in earnest this evening. Gus swaped old gray off to day. Got a splendid little gray mare. She is a little spoilt but wont pitch. She only prances. I think made a good trade. He gave some boot. I wrote two articles of agreement to day for Adare, one between Adare + Near. Also drew a note for 8 yearlings.[45] The other men that came for cattle still here. Tis night cattle pened.

[*page 85*] *Wednesday September 16th 1868*

Wind blew hard and cold all night. Cloudy this morning. Fixing to cut out cattle for Badford + Doctor Crawford. Looks like clearing off. Finished cutting out. Wrote article of agreement. Signed + + Some of the boys gone to Earharts to cut out some cattle out of his herd that they brought through. Wind still high + cold. Dont Sanders traded for a saddle to day. Had to run

45. That Adare asked Bailey to write two business agreements and a note suggests that Bailey may have had more education than Adare.

back. Dispute between him + Adare about the cow he gave to boot. She was picked up as we came through by Sanders. Adare told the men Dont had no right to sell her, so they wouldent take her. Sanders wouldent give them another. He says Adare will sell her if he gets a chance. Of course he will. Joe Martin quit us to day. Gone with [Frank?] Martin to Fall River. I close for to day. Boys bringing in the cattle.

[*page 86*] *Thursday September 17th 1868*

All right this morning. Witts pony fell with him while runing a cow and fell on his leg but accidently dident hurt him much. He got his foot fastened in the stirup + had to hold the mare down til he got help. 12 oclock. Been separateing the Beef + stock cattle all day. The beef to to [go] to market Stock to let on shares. Cut out a small beef to kill. Drove it to camp. While Mart Bean + Reagan was herding their cattle to day their camp caught fire + burned up everything they had at camp.[46] Earhart got his cattle out of our herd. Bud + I are herding for the boys to get dinner. Bean + Reagan will have a hard time without blankets to cover with. We havent enought to divide with them. Had some frost this morning. Gus staked his mare last night. This morning she is gone this morning. Guess she will go back to her old range + colt, ++

46. Reagan probably was James Reagan of Jack County, Texas. His name appears on the 1860 U.S. census rolls for Jack County along with a wife and five young children. He listed his occupation as "raising cattle." James Reagan would have been thirty-seven in 1868, the same age as Bailey.

[page 87] Friday September 18th 1868

I had a severe pain in my side last night. It kept me awake all night. It is a pleuresy pain. All hands come to the conclusion that there is a bunch of stears gone, in fact we can miss some noted stears. Lewis was on herd when they left but they say it was not carelesnes in him. No sir a negroe dont get careless. If it had been any of the white boys they would say neglect, at once but as it is Lewis'es fault it is all right..so say I. Adare + Witt is gone hunting for the cattle. I dont care if they dont find them. They like to have got mad at me because I said Lewis + Ben went to sleep. They got back. Dident find any cattle. Witt gone again. John Adare gone to Sheltons boys. All on herd. Adare traded for a mare. A Mexican came to camp. He lives on Walnut. Some men came 30 miles to trade for cattle all rideing bareback. One of them had on a new hat, Broad cloth coat, black *[page 88]* pants, brogan shoes run down. No socks. Pants four or six inches too short. Had on gloves rideing on a bed quilt and blind bridle. I recon he has some money. He had to leave without effecting a trade. Will be back he says. There is a norther comeing up so he has to take the quilt home. I dont look for him 'til it turns warm.

Saturday Sep 19th 1868

All up this morning. Adares mare got loose last night. Gone after her now. Gus is gone after his mare too. They are haveing a hard time of it with their new horses. Boys haveing plenty fun over it. They dident find any beef yesterday. Witt gone again to day. Adare got back with his mare. Witt has got in. Found some of the runaway stears. Gus has got in with his mare too. All in now. No more today. Cattle in for the night.

[*page 89*] *Sunday September 20th 1868*

Had a hard rain last night, all up this morning. Gus + John gone to the tradeing house for flour. Bean from Cook County here to day. Got here very hungry. Says hea has had nothing to eat for 2 ½ days. Left their herd at Arks River. Are after grub. I am pestered to day with rheumatism. I dont feel well at all. Several of the boys complaining to day. All in camp.

Monday September 21st 1868

All up this morning. Nothing going on around camp. I dont know when we will get away from here. We have set several days to start + been disappointed as often. More men here to day after cattle to keep on shares. McCabe is her trying to buy some cattle. Went huck berry hunting to day. Got a fine chance. All in for the night.

[*page 90*] *Tuesday September the 22nd 1868*

Our hack berrys gave all of us the whats name last night. John Adare took on awfully awhile. He thought he was going to die. No such luck. All strait this morning. Just before day the wind came from the north in a whiz. Suppose it is an equinoctial gale had company last night. Move our tents to day about 200 yds on account of the wind. Find it much more pleasant. We are in the bend of the creek timber all north of us. Plenty wood handy. Wind cant strike us. I have had a severe pain in my shoulder all day. Adare + Bud Ham are gone after hay to put in our tents. Our men left this evening. They will be back this week. All moved and fixed up. 'Tis very cold. Rounding up to pen for the night. Supper is preparing.

[*page 91*] *Wednesday September 23rd 1868*

I am sick to day. You bet I would like to be at home. My side + shoulder kept me awake all night. I took some pills last night which operated finely. Hope I will be better when they work off. Bud has just come in with two fine turkeys which he killed with his pistole. I am so lonesome. My pills make me so sick. I am out of sorts + mad because I was such a fool to come this trip and contrary to the wishes of my wife an ad[v]ise of good friends but I thought I could stand it. I dont know whether I will get well or not, but I bet I will. I have strong symtoms of pneumonia. One consolation is that I am not afraid to die. I am just as well taken care of as a person could be as far as being kept comfortable + my wants supplyed is concerned. Mrs Adare + Annie are very good + kind to me. I am no better now.

[*page 92*] *Thursday September the 24th 1868*

I was very sick all night am some better this morning have a low dull fever. I believe if I had a Doctor an plenty medicine I could make a die of it, but as I have neither there is a chance for me to get well.[47] John Squares got to our camp today was very glad to hear from home but I was sorry when he told me he had no letter for me from my wife.[48] It is our calculation to leave here tomorrow or next day. Had sleet yesterday and rain nearly all night. Still (Mizling as Luke Shoat says). Killing a beef to day boys shot at it several time it started up the hill Dont Sanders caught it by the tail + slam him gin de ground. Got it killed at last had to drag it from the pen with oxen. Clouds look broken all in for the night. I hope I will rest better to night.

[*page* 93] *Friday September the 25*

Looks like clearing off this morning. Hope it will. Reagan came over last night. I gave him a dose of medicine. He was very sick all night. Took cramp in his bowels just before day. I rested very well all night. Bud shot a

47. Bailey seems to have had little confidence in medical doctors and their medicines. On the frontier not all doctors were trusted. In addition, because doctors were scarce, many people relied heavily on home remedies and believed in letting the human body heal itself.

48. John Squares is probably John W. Squires of Parker County, Texas. Squires, a native of Louisiana and an original landowner in Jack County, was a Jacksboro merchant in 1860. On June 25, 1866, he was elected sheriff of Jack County. In the turmoil of Reconstruction in Texas following the Civil War, Squires and hundreds of other elected county officials across Texas were removed from office by Gen. J. J. Reynolds. Reynolds issued Special Order #195 following complaints from Unionists, blacks, and others that elected officials refused to protect their lives and property. Why John Squires, forty-one, arrived in Bailey's camp from Texas is unclear, but he may have had a financial interest in the herd. Bailey later writes that Squires was going with Adare and the remaining cattle to Abilene.

wolf. Ran it about one mile. Saw it was wounded. Run it in Some bushes. Shot it again + killed it the first shot. Was close to the pen. Cattle got scared. Had a considerable run in the correlle but dident break out. Another old head here after cattle. Have let him take a lot to keep til spring. Nothing else to day. Squares is still with us. Is after money. Will stay until sales are made. All up this evening. Night.

[*page 94*] *Saturday Sept 26th 1868*

Appearance of rain this morning. I rested bully last night. All fixing to leave here. Every body anxious to get away from here. I dont much believe we will get off to day. Boys are cuting out cattle and arangeing herd to get off. Shure enough not ready to start. Night now. <u>I gues we will start tomorrow.</u>

Sunday September 27th 1868

I rested well again last night. Again I believe I am nearly well. We will get off this morning. The crowd splits here. Part goes to Abaline balence to Lawrence. I will go to Lawrence with the families. John Squires goes with the cattle to Abaline. I will close my record so far as the cattle is concerned. It is one hundred + ten miles to Abaline [*page 95*] and about 160 to Lawrence. I am glad to get rid of driveing. Bud Ham John Adare + Charlie will go to Lawrence. Bud + John goes to help the old fellow with the cattle he got home. They will meet us at Emporia. Mrs Adare drives one wagon. Charlie the other.

I am horseback. I am about 2 miles ahead of the Waggons, resting under an elm on Walnut. There is four new houses in sight. Walnut is very thickly settled so I am told. One thing it is a very pretty and good country. Waggons came up. Nooned on the creek. McCabe passed us going up to Eldarado. One of his horses gave out. Hired another. Bean come to use on his way from Mill. He is going to the herd. Start, travel up the creek 18 miles to Junction Store.[49] Stop for the night.

[*page 96*] *Monday Sept the 28th*

We are at the junction of Whitewater one of the pretiest creeks I ever saw. Are in sight of Dr. Stewarts formerly of Wise County.[50] This is in a thick settled country, and by the by one of the best countrys I have seen since I left Texas. Some of the pretiest valleys I ever saw. Plenty water grass + timber. We got some flour meat + Irish potatoes. Rained on us last night. I got wet consequently. I have

49. The Junction Store was operated by L. Shamleffer, formerly of Council Grove, Kansas, and C. N. James. Soon after this area of southern Kansas was opened for settlement early in 1868, Shamleffer and James purchased a claim for forty dollars and constructed a log building. They opened it as a trading post in July 1868, just a few months before Bailey and others on the cattle drive arrived. The store was located at the junction of the Whitewater River and the Walnut River. It was the first building in what is today Augusta, Kansas, named for C. N. James's wife.

50. Thomas Stewart, physician, listed in the 1860 U.S. census for Wise County. A native of Pennsylvania, Stewart moved west to Illinois, married, and moved on to Texas about 1858, settling in Wise County. At the start of the Civil War, he moved his family to Kansas. He was the father of six children. The 1870 U.S. census lists a Thomas Stewart living in Augusta Township, Butler County.

the pain in my side again. Fixing to start. Roads very muddy. Came 16 miles to day. Got to Eldarado a little town situated on Walnut Creek. A new place it is the county seat of Butler County. Dist[rict] Court is going on at this time. I dont think there is an over flow of tallent amongst the lawyers. The place is built up of plank [*page* 97] houses, principally black houses. It is in a beautiful valley a pretty situation for a town. Have company to night. Got here sometime before night ~~came 16 ms to day~~ [*preceding phrase crossed out*]. They have a little steam mill here all out of doors, but seems to be pecking away. Cleared off.

Tuesday September 29th 1868

We all done fine last night. Had a splendid place to camp, camped in the bottom under some large hackberrys. Plenty wood + water. Got some meal at the mill to feed on. A Mr Langly + his lady came to our camp last night + set 'til bed time. He lives here. Dr. Steward + Brandon took breakfast with us this morning. Waggons started. Noon on a branch of Walnut. An old man is building a house in the bank of the creek. Two families 6 [*page* 98] from Iowa nooning here. They are down on the country. Start 2 oclock. Camp on head of Walnut at a large Spring. Has a name but I have forgotten it.

Wednesday Sept 30th

Done fine last night. After we stoped a man from Emporia stoped to camp also. He has a wagon. Gave us a peach a peace. An old Dutch woman came to camp with som turnups the largest I ever saw. Bought them. She is down on Kansas. I use her own language. It is the d - n - st country she ever saw + says she will be d - ned if she dont leave it before long. Nooned on branch 200 yds to right of road. Got corn at Norton's on south fork of Cottonwood creek. Crossed some beautiful little creeks to day several small farms. Have not passed a [*page 99*] field with more than 20 acres in cultivation. Land seems to be rich but subject to drouth. Crops very sorry in this whole country. Lake up for the night.

Thursday October the 1st 1868

Rained all night but we kep dry. It was dark + raining when we stoped. Women mad + quarreling. Children crying. Looked like a storm comeing on us but turned off to a study hard rain. But we are all right this morning. The women slept off their mad. It is foggy. I have to go back one mile to pay for corn. We couldent make change last night. This part of the country is not so good. I think Texas lays over it in every particular. I have not seen a double house in Kansas.[51] Hardly any of them have chimneys. Fenceing is very sorry. Made of three rails to the panel. [*page 100*] Roads are very mudy to day. In five

51. Double house: a so-called Texas house, a structure that consists of two houses or two sets of rooms semi-annexed to each other by a connecting roof over a long hall open on two sides. Texans called the open space under the roof a dog-trot. These breezeways were usually set to catch the prevailing winds. Such houses were appropriate to most areas of Texas where winters are normally mild, but they were not suitable in Kansas where winters are often severe.

miles of Emporia came to Cotton wood a large creek bottom very muddy an boggy. Got to Emporia Sundown. Meet John + Bud. Take up for the night. It is all a nortion about men working so much harder than Texan people. Their houses are not as large. (I speak of country houses.) Fences nothing to compare but they say it is easier to herd stock out than it is to build fences. Tis true they raise some vegitables here, but I cant see but we live as well in Texas as they do here. We are at Newt Nixes an old Jack County neighbor.[52]

Friday October the 2nd

Spent the night very agreeably with Nix + family. One consolation. I dont see how Mrs Adare's tounge can run to day if she dident talk last [*page 101*] night. I couldent hear if all she told was true. She would be a thunderin old woman, rich aint no name for it. Made milions since she saw Nix. Nix + wife appeared glad to see us + I recon glad to see us start though. As a matter of courtesy asked us very easy to lay over a day. I am siting in Drug Store in Emporia writeing.[53] Emporia is about as large as

52. The 1858 and 1859 tax rolls for Jack County, Texas, contain the name Newton Nix. The 1870 census roll for Lyon County, Kansas, lists Newton T. Nix, thirty-nine, a native of Illinois, his wife Polina, thirty-six, from Kentucky, and four children: Virginia, age thirteen; Florinda, age nine; Edward, age four; and Mary A., age two. Texas is listed as the birthplace of all four children.

53. Emporia, Lyon County, Kansas, is located about fifty-five miles northeast of El Dorado. To reach Emporia, Bailey would have traveled across a portion of Chase County, Kansas, and the Flint Hills. In all likelihood Moses H. Bates, a native of Indiana, operated the Emporia drugstore, where Bailey wrote

Weatherford, a very flourishing place, in the prairie.[54] No timber nearer than 3 miles. Water by diging. Bud gone to see if we can cross the Neotio river.[55] Start at 11 oclock. Bought ½ bushel apples and other notions. Came out three miles to Neotio. Nooning. River low. Had to come 13 miles this evening to get wood. Got to a good place.

[*page 102*] *Saturday Oct 3d 1868*

Done fine last night, some appearance of rain this morning. Came 3 miles to a large creek. Good farm and a fine frame house. The largest field and house I have seen. Country improveing in looks and seem to be more at work than back apeace. Got my bridle broke all to peaces this morning. Came 5 miles. Got to Burlingame, County seat of Osage County.[56] After crossing several pretty little streams came to a large hous on a creek. Has lots of sheep. Well fixed. Got corn. Stoped to camp several

---

an entry in his journal. Bates moved to Emporia, Kansas, in 1861 and started the first drugstore in the town. In 1868 Bates would have been twenty-nine.

54. Weatherford, Texas, located thirty miles west of Fort Worth. The town was incorporated in 1858, and a post office was opened in 1859. From 1858 to 1868 Weatherford was considered a safe haven for nearby residents, who fled to the town during Indian raids. The town was midway on the stage line between Fort Worth and Fort Belknap. Weatherford was named for Jefferson Weatherford, a member of the Texas Senate.

55. The Neosho River, which enters northwest Lyon County, Kansas, and passes north of Emporia as it flows southeast.

56. Bailey probably traveled north from Emporia, Kansas, to the old Santa Fe Trail, which ran from the northeast to the southwest across Kansas. He turned east and followed the old trail to Burlingame, located in northwest Osage County, Kansas. Burlingame was a stop on the Santa Fe Trail until railroads replaced freight wagons and traffic on the trail declined.

hundred yds to left of road. Wood scarce. Good grass and water. Stoped in town a while. Got flour at the mill. One of the finest mills in the state. It is right in the center of town. Several large substantial brick buildings here. Came 7 ms to a creek to camp.

[*page 103*] *Sunday October the 4th 1868*

All passed off well last night. Ready to start. This is a beautiful morning. We are in 33 miles of Lawrence. Came 8 miles to a small viliage one store, hotel, livery, stable, + a church one or two other houses. Town called Ridgeway, a very appropriate name.[57] It is situated on a high prairie ridge. Country very broken. Came 6 miles to another viliage. Only a church + tavern. Some other buildings going up. They call it Twin Mouns.[58] Been trying to get bacon all day. Cant hear of any. I dont see what people eat in this country. After passing another viliage (Clinton) Stoped to noon on a muddy branch. Cross a high well finished bridge at Sigle post office.[59] Get corn here. Stop to camp.

57. Ridgeway was located in northern Osage County, Kansas, on the Santa Fe Trail. Clinton is a small community located in Douglas County, about nine miles southwest of Lawrence.

58. Twin Mound was a small community located southwest of Clinton near the western edge of Douglas County, Kansas. Henry Hiatt built his home there in 1858, constructed a gristmill, and attempted to establish a town. A post office opened in June 1858, but was discontinued in 1900. As a town, Twin Mound never developed. Today the town site is under Clinton Lake, southwest of Lawrence, Kansas.

59. Bailey's mention of Clinton as a stopping point suggests that Bailey and his party left the Santa Fe Trail about seven miles south of Clinton to

[*page 104*] *Monday October 5*

We are in Seven Miles of Lawrence. Adare left us yesterday morning to go on to procure a house.[60] Start. Well we are in the citty of Lawrence haveing lots of fun. I believe Bud will laugh himself to death. Just as we got in town three or four of the children took the trots. You ought to hear the old lady rare. She wants to put on style. Well she does with a vengence. I + Bud are going up in town to hunt Adare. Children have to get out on the street. Noon on street. Adare got a little hous to. Into it this evening. In it + night.

Tuesday October the 6th 1868

Took breakfast in a house in town this morning. Got with Hardin + Earhart to day. Had a fine [*page 105*] time. I cant tell when I will start home. I + Earhart eat in what is called the kija hole. A house under the ground. We cant see much of Quantrells sign here.[61] He burnt this place down during the war. I can see several cripples he + his men made at the time. They say he got lots of money.

---

travel north to Lawrence. The Santa Fe Trail ran south of Lawrence. Sigel was a farming community located in the Wakarusa River valley about four miles southwest of Lawrence in Douglas County, Kansas. The post office Bailey observed was established on December 20, 1862, but discontinued in 1896.

60. Adare probably planned to spend some time in Lawrence, but no evidence has been found to suggest that he and his family made their home there.

61. William Clarke Quantrill, the Confederate guerrilla who raided Lawrence, August 21, 1863. He and his men burned much of the town, killed about one hundred fifty people, and wounded many others.

Tuesday [Wednesday] October 7th

I start for home to day. I am going with Jim Harding.[62] Waiting now for him to come in after me. He went out about 6 miles last night. I start lo for Texas. Good by folks came out 7 miles. Camp on a large creek. Toll bridge over it.[63] Came up with Reagan + Bean. Camped with them, also Christian boys. The Christians are going through to Texas with us.[64]

[*page 106*] *Thursday October 8th*

I rested bully last night. Roll out in earnest for Texas this morning. There is four of us in croud. Now a jolly little crowd. Started in a gallop. Got 4 waggons along good teams. Splendid road to start off on. Came 12 miles. Stoped to noon. Geting along finely. Have lots of fun holering for Seymore + singing.[65] The people dont seem to relish it much. Came 12 miles this evening. Stoped to camp at Otway a town at the end of railroad callew [*sp?*].

62. Jim Harding may have been Jesse Harding, a Jack County, Texas, cattle raiser. A native of New York, he is listed on the 1860 U.S. census for Jack County, Texas. He was married and had three daughters. He would have been fifty-two in 1868. His full name is believed to have been Jesse James Harding.

63. The bridge mentioned by Bailey crossed the Wakarusa River near Lawrence.

64. Perhaps the sons of Ben Christian, who ran a hotel in Sherman, Texas, and who was supposedly a friend of William Clarke Quantrill (see note 61). Tom and Bone Christian, mentioned in Bailey's journal entries, were brothers. It is not known if Tom Christian actually rode with Quantrill and his band, as Bailey believed. Tom Christian's name does not appear on known lists of those who were with Quantrill.

65. "Hollering for Seymore" seems to be Bailey's phrase meaning everyone was feeling happy and having a good time.

Situated on Mary Mazine.[66] A large creek, fine tool bridge + + it is a very flourishing place. The bridge is a suspension bridge. Camp in edge of town. There seems to be considerable wealth in this country and a great deal of aristocracy. Everything seems to be progressive.

[*page 107*] *Friday October 9th 1868*

Our horses are gone this morning or part of them. Harding + Tom Christian gone after them. Returned with horses. Followed back 5 ms. Start 9 oclock. Stoped in town. I + Harding purchased several little articles such as candy preserved peaches + + for our families. Came out thirteen miles. Came to Iowa Citty a small place.[67] Stoped to noon on a creek. Jim has the sick head ache very bad. Is subject to such spells. Stay here til morning.

Saturday October 10th 1868

Got a very early start this morning came 5 miles to Garnett a flourishing little place 5 busines houses + town improveing. Came 30 miles to day nothing hapened through the day [*page 108*] worthy of note. Stoped on the

66. "Otway" is Ottawa, Kansas, the county seat of Franklin County, Kansas. "Mary Mazine" is the Marais du Cygne River, which begins in southern Wabaunsee County, Kansas, and flows to the east and southeast across Kansas. It empties into the Osage River on the boundary between Bates and Vernon Counties in Missouri.

67. No historical records have been located concerning a community called Iowa City located five miles north of Garnett, Kansas, in 1868. Bailey is probably referring to the settlement of Scipio, which in 1868 was located five miles north of Garnett.

prairie. No wood in sight. Got wood to cook with at a house. The old man cant talk, (in a horn).

Sunday, October the 11th 1868

All right this morning. I got on a horse went to a house got 4 day eggs for breakfast. The old man came to camp last night. Talked us all to sleep about 12 oclock. We rized him pretty heavy about his radical principals. Said he was radical. He hears some great tales about Rebels in Texas. We dident tell him any beter. Told him Texas was a hot place for his sort. This is a beautiful morning. Came 8 miles to Maypleton a town on Osage Creek.[68] Came 3 miles to a branch. Eat 2 water melons for diner. Came 12 miles. Got corn [*page 109*] at $1.00 per bushel. Stoped to camp on a branch in sight of old Ft. Scott. Met a waggon full of women this eveing. They laughed at Jim Harding. He snorted at them. Raised a big laugh. Roads are the best I ever saw. Country very thickly settle. Passed a parcel of men around a little bunch of Texas beef in the act of shooting them on the prairie. They killed a pen full at Moun Citty the other day.[69]

68. The town of Mapleton was located in northern Bourbon County, Kansas. Originally called Eldora, it was renamed Mapleton in 1857. It was located about twelve miles northwest of Fort Scott, Kansas, a military post established in 1842. Fort Scott was active during the abolitionist period until 1855, again from 1862 to 1865 during the Civil War, and from 1870 to 1875 during Reconstruction. The town of Fort Scott, about four miles from the western border of Missouri, grew up around the military post.

69. Mound City, Kansas, located twenty miles north-northwest of Fort Scott.

They swear people shant drive through the country. If the law dont stop it, they will. Let um rip.

Monday October the 12th 1868

All right this morning. Only old Grant is out of the way. (He is an old flea biten gray poon, sore back + one eyed horse.) I named him Grant. Found him. Came 3 miles to Ft Scott. It is a fast place. Stoped + got some goods. [*page 110*] Goods of all description cheaper than in Lawrence. Came six ms. Came to creek. Nooned. Came 5 miles to Wheeling on the line between Kansas + Missouri. Line runs through the center of town. Not much place. Came to a little town + camped. I dont know the name of it yet.

Tuesday October the 13th 1868

All up this morning ready to start. Noon at stage stand. Not a stick of timber in sight. Have to make coffee by a weed fire. Does very well. Houses been scarse to day. Are on what is called Line road. A great deal of travel done on this road. Stoped to buy corn. A little boy came out. We got to deviling him. He got so perplexed he couldent count the money. He had to go to the field after the old man. Kept us half hour [*page 111*] dident make much that time. We are now what is called Neutral land, a good + beautiful country but no timeber. Not much settlement on it. It is in dispute with the Osage Indians. They claim it + I recon it is theirs. Camp on Cow Creek at another little town.

Wednesday, Oct 14 1868

Rained last night. All kept dry, though looks like rain this morning. Noon on a creek four miles from Baxter Springs.[70] A Doctor Foot + Jim McGill took diner with us. Had Oysters + crackers for diner. Foot was tight. Got to Baxter, Got several little necessaries. Came one mile. Camp. Got corn at the springs, going back to town to night.

[page 112] Wednesday, October [crossed out]
Thursday October 15th 1868

Tom Mahaffy formely of Wise City Spent the night with us last night.[71] Went back to Town last night + heard a radical speech by Vos of Kansas.[72] There was an old man got with us at camp. Went with us to the speaking. We put him up to asking the man questions. We stamped for him every time and he + us together bothered Vos so he had to quit. Then the police got after us and we had to

70. Baxter Springs is located in southeast Kansas just north of the Oklahoma border. It was named for John Baxter, an early settler. In 1866, and again from 1870 through 1879, it was a cattle town. To comply with Kansas laws prohibiting Texas cattle from being driven through that part of the state, cattle pens were constructed just south of Baxter Springs in Indian Territory. Beginning in 1870 Texas cattle were loaded into railroad cars in Indian Territory and shipped by rail through Kansas. It was not against Kansas law to ship Texas cattle by rail.

71. Tom Mahaffy probably is H. T. Mahaffie, who is listed in the 1860 U.S. census for Wise County, Texas. In 1868 Mahaffie would have been twenty-four.

72. Most likely Kansas State Senator M. V. Voss of Fort Scott, a native of Ohio and an attorney. He would have been twenty-nine in 1868. Voss later became a district judge in Kansas.

git We would have led them a lively string if they had followed us to camp. We heard they were coming. I sent word for them to come. There were about 20 Texians at camp all cw [Civil War] men and well armed. We would clean them up for awhile.[73] All start.

[*page 113*] *Friday October th 16th 1868*

Rained on us all night. An old fellow took dinner with us to day. It is still raining. Start early. Nooned at forks of road. Met some families moveing from Cook Co. Texas. Came to Senica Citty a little vilage in Newton County Missouri.[74] Now in Sinica Nation. Had a chicken for diner oysters crackers + + came to an Indian settlement the Senica Tribe with a few scatering Wyandots. Fine large looking Indians. We are in Senica haveing a waggon worked on. Several standing around asking questions about Texas + + been raining all day. Every thing is wet though I have kept tolerable dry. Came out 5 ms. Camp for to night, Night.

[*page 114*] *Saturday Oct 17th 1868*

Got an early start this morning. Come five miles. Overtook several familys going to Texas. Some going to Missouri. Passed several waggons loade[d] with apples

73. Bailey was obviously bluffing when he sent word to town that there were twenty well-armed Texans waiting. His bluff worked.

74. Soon after leaving Fort Scott, Bailey crossed into Missouri and headed south. "Senica Citty" is the town of Seneca, Missouri, located almost on the border of eastern Oklahoma, then Indian Territory.

for Texas. Noon at store on Honey creek. I dont know what its name originated from. Came seven miles to Maysville, Arkansas.[75] Can see lots of war sign all through this country. We havent passed a plantation to day but there is an old chimney standing. House was burned. Every house in Maysville was burned down.[76] They have built up again. There is three dry good establishments two drug stores and a family grocery in the place. Several dwelling houses we are in Benton County, said to be the best county in the state, and it is for rocks. I never saw a rocky a country in my life. Came out seven or eight [*page 115*] miles to Wiley McFaddins an old citizen. He was burnt out during the war. We camp here to night. He has the finest apple orchard I ever saw. Corn is good through here. Vegitables any amount. This is a good farming country if you can get below the rocks, but in the valleys

75. Honey Creek runs northwest to southeast across the eastern border of Kansas, the southwestern tip of Missouri, and into Arkansas. The store mentioned by Bailey may have been just north of present-day Southwest City, Missouri, or just across the nearby state line in Arkansas. The distance from where Honey Creek enters Arkansas to Maysville is much greater than seven miles. Maysville is located west of modern Gravette (see note 76).

76. Maysville is located in Benton County, northwest Arkansas, not far from the Civil War battlefield at Pea Ridge and the Elkhorn Saloon, about five miles south of the Missouri border, where Union forces defeated Confederate troops in March 1862. Although the Confederate forces then left the area, they returned early in the fall of 1862. Just outside of Maysville Union troops attacked a small force of Confederates who retreated. The struggle involved considerable destruction of private property. Between April and late September, there was no law and order in northwest Arkansas. Deserters and stragglers from both armies and local criminals ravaged and burned many homes, causing much of the damage seen by Bailey in Maysville.

ground is rich. Looks like a healthy country. Camp. Mrs. McFadin sends us out a large dish of white head cabbage for supper also some stewed apples.

Sunday October the 18th 1868

Had a big rain last night but dident get wet. We slept in the crib. Had a fine time. Chickens roasted [roosted] over us. We dident know it 'til in the night. There was six or eight hound dogs in the crib too. Kept me awake nearly all night. Still raining this morning. It is our intention to stay here in this [*page 116*] neighborhood three or four days. Tom Christian has gone over to see his wife. They have been parted about one year. I think Tom is going to try to fix it up with her. He says it was all [h]is fault, so say the neighbors. She lives 10 miles from here at her fathers. He is brother to McFadins. His name too. I dont know how he will make it. Bone, (Toms brother) says he dont believe she will fix it up. I bet him the cider she would. Young McFadin invited us to breakfast with him. Of course we accepted + made up for lost time you. He had a splendid breakfast. His wife is a nice woman. Well here come Tom with his <u>frau</u> (wife) all fixed up She is a good looking woman. Tom is a wild boy. He was in Quantrells outfit during the war. Married since the war closed. I had fun this morning out of one of McFadins sons, a grown young man. I asked him what country we are in. [*page 117*] He studied awhile. At last he said, well, well, I believe folks call it Arkansaw but he dident know whether it is named that or not. Said his brother is in the house. He could tell if I would wait and ask him. Appearance of rain. Tis night.

Monday October 18th 1868

Rained all night last night. We came over to Tom's wife's house yesterday. Stayed in the house last night. Had a good supper good bed, good breakfast, consequently I feel very good this morning. In comeing 10 miles yesterday we traveled 15 at least going around hills + + traveled about two miles in Coon holler. Got percimons grapes and hazle nuts in abundance. Tom + Jim Harding are gone this morning to see about buying some apples. Gone to Col Hastings. Old Grant is gone this morning. Boys returned from Hastings. Will get apples from him at 40c per bushel, currency. [*page 118*] We will go over ther tomorrow if it dont rain too much. We will stay here until it clears off. I want to get off for home, but I cant tell when we will get off. Benton is a great county for apples. Have apple dumplins for diner. I found it out at breakfast so I touched breakfast light saveing for diner but it is pleaged [pledged] late. We are fixing for night.

Tuesday October the 20th 1868

Raining yet, got breakfast, went to the blacksmith shop three miles, to get some shoeing done. It has rained the day out. We were going to load to day but rain prevented us, <u>rain</u>, <u>rain</u>, <u>rain</u>, Got back about 2 oclock. Had a splendid diner, sweet potatoes, Irish potatoes green apple pies turnups pickles + splendid coffee. Good God how I want to start home. Here is night again so turn in, old Grant out yet.

[*page 119*] *Wednesday, October th 21st 1868*

Some appearance of clearing off this morning. Wind comeing with a whiz from the north. Still at old McF. The old lady amuses me telling her troubles and scrapes during the war. She was one of the strongest of southern women. She burryed 2 of her sons that was shot close to the house and Tom Christian's wife burryed her husband. He was killed one mile from home. She hunted him three days before she found him. (She was a widdow when Tom married her.) The jayhawkers killed him + showed her part of his clothes and his pistole. While they, (on one of the men) was showing her his six shooter clinch west slised up + shot him through the heart or near it. Kill him immediately so she got the pistole. The old lady says they killed one of her little boys aged 11 years for nothing. She says he oldest son. Razed them up though glory in [*page 120*] his spunk. Tells me she has rode 10 + 15 miles lots of nights to let southern boys know the Rads were in. They broke the old man clear up, burnt him out. I am very lonesome to day. We will drive over to Hastings this evening as as soon as we can gear up. We aim to start tomorrow for Texas, if it dont rain.

Thursday October the 22nd 1868

At the orchard. Came over yesterday evening + loaded 24 bushels on one wagon. It is harder work than I bargained for. Some of the finest largest + redest apples I ever saw. Nothing pretier than an apple orchard of large ripe fruit. I think by working hard we will make a start this evening for home. Old Phoenix Formely of Jack County came to camp to day. Have not seen him for seven or eight years. [*page 121*] He has settled in this county. Is not pleased. Says he is bound to go back to Texas next spring. Dont blame him. Apples are silling from 30 to 50 cts per bushel, according to quality. Kentucky reds, highest, next Water core, next Royal Reds, next Milams + so on. I dont know all the different knds. Old Grant is gone yet. Bone is fixing to get off without him. Old McFaddin is going with us. Ready to start. Came out 2 miles to the road. Old Mc + Tom gone home. We camp at this place to night. Harding gone after chickens + potatoes about 2 mile.

Friday October the 23d 1868

All right this morning, Tom and Old Mc has got back to camp. Had chicken for supper + breakfast. Got off 9 oclock. Came about 10 miles. Tom though he heard of Old Grant. Is gone back for him. I have no idea it is him he hear of. [*page 122*] Came 16 mile to Heldebrands Mill in the nation on the line road.[77] Tom not overtaken us yet. A great many Indians about the mill. Came 2 miles. Struck camp. Find spring 200 yds to left of road

77. Hildebrand's mill was located five miles west of the Arkansas line in the Cherokee Nation, Indian Territory. Its location today is in northern Adair County, Oklahoma, east of Tahlequah.

The mill is on a beautiful runing creek. It is a fine mill, steam. We got 50 [lbs.?] flour + some bacon at last. This is a very mountainous country. We are between 2 large mountains. Have been nearly all evening. Road runs down a pas several miles. Close for the night.

Saturday, October the 24th 1868

A fellow from Grayson County Texas camped with us last night. I dream so much about my little Charlie boy. I cant help but feel uneasy. I dreamed last night he was very sick. I dont believe in dreams but cant help from thinking something rong. Wish I was at home with my wife and [*page 123*] little boys. Two of our horses are out of the way this morning. I went one end of the road. Jim Harding the other. I have got back. I hear Jim shoot he has found them. Tom Christian has gone back to take another hunt for Grant. Met folks moveing from Texas Navaro County, going to Washington Coty Arkansas.[78] Get no corn tonight. Not much grass + very little water. Muddy at that, we have passed over a very rough rocky country especially Spring Creek hill which is about six miles across it.

Sunday October th 25 1868

Before leaving camp this morning Beadle from Parker County drove up to camp on his way home. Says he will

78. Navaro County is located in east-central Texas. Washington County, Arkansas, is the next county south of Benton County, Arkansas.

wait for us at Ft Scott.[79] Tom Christian got in again last night about midnight but no Grant yet, so we have to leave him. Not much loss. [*page 124*] Nearly all the horses are gone this morning. I am afraid the Indians have driven them off. Ther was two or three passed the camp about dark. One of them stoped and eat supper. Asked a great many questions + left. We hear to day he is a suspicious character. Heard of the horses seven miles back. Bone + Harding gone back. They are comeing. We are fixing diner. To eat a snack before starting as it is nearly dinner time. Got off at 2 oclock. Had to come 12 miles this evening to get feed for horses. Passed through Tulaqua a litte town.[80] Several white men in it doing business. We are in Cherokee Nation. A great many Negroes liveing in this nation. Got with a man named Daraty in town from Grayson County on his way home.[81] Been to

79. Perhaps one of two sons of W. Beadle, a farmer, whose name appears in the 1860 U.S. census for Parker County. In 1868 he would have been sixty and probably too old to make the trail drive. One of his sons would have been twenty-eight, the other twenty-six years old in 1868. Both sons were born in Tennessee and moved to Texas with the family in the late 1850s. Beadle telling Bailey that he would see him in Fort Scott is a mystery. Bailey had already passed through Fort Scott, Kansas, on his journey home. It might indicate that Bailey planned to return to Kansas later, but no evidence of this has been found.

80. Tahlequah, Oklahoma, the Cherokee capital in Indian Territory. Bailey's journal suggests that after he left Washington County, Arkansas, he traveled southwest into Indian Territory and to Tahlequah, whose name comes from a Cherokee word, *talikwa* or *tellico,* meaning "an old Cherokee town."

81. Probably James M. Daugherty, born in Texas County, Missouri, on February 27, 1850. Daugherty grew up in Texas. At age sixteen, with five other cowboys, he drove his first herd of Texas cattle to Missouri, only to be stopped and whipped by border ruffians. He drove his cattle back into Indian Territory

Missouri with cattle. Has his family along also a boy from Tarran County Texas.[82] [*page 125*] We will travel together. Hope so at least. He is very anxious to go in company with us. It is not considered very safe for a man to travel alone through this country.

Monday October th 26th 1868

Got a very ealy start this morning. Pass the Cherokee Seminary a large three story hous, a beautiful location for a school.[83] Came 5 miles to a very fine large spring. Forgot the name of it. It is rather a noted place. Came 12 ½ miles to a little runing creek. Stoped to noon. We have met a great many Indians to day. Corn is very scarse along the road. Have passed over a rich country to day, and shows that it was once a fast country but was tore up during the war. Nearly all timber got to Fort Gibson.[84] A very good looking place but has appearance of a great

---

but soon arranged their sale to a Fort Scott, Kansas, cattle buyer. Daugherty took many other herds of Texas cattle to Kansas and Missouri during the years that followed. By the 1920s he was known as "Uncle Jim Daugherty" and owned a large ranch spanning Culberson and Hudspeth Counties, Texas. In 1923 he wrote his trail-driving recollections; see J. Marvin Hunter, compiler and editor, *The Trail Drivers of Texas* (San Antonio: Jackson Printing Co., 1923), vol. 2, pp. 137–40.

82. Tarrant County, Texas, where Fort Worth is located.

83. The Cherokee Seminary was established in 1846 at Tahlequah. In 1909 the Oklahoma state legislature purchased the seminary. It is today Northeastern State University.

84. Fort Gibson, located on the Grand or Neosho River three miles above its junction with the Arkansas River, is in Muskogee County, Oklahoma. First called Cantonment Gibson, it was renamed Fort Gibson on April 21, 1824, in honor of Col. George Gibson, head of the Army Commissary Department.

The Cherokee Female Seminary in Tahlequah, which Jack Bailey passed in 1868 as he was returning to Texas. Courtesy Western History Collections, University of Oklahoma Libraries.

deal of poverty especially among the Negroes which I believe is the largest part of the community. US troops are [*page 126*] stationed her. This post is a good looking place. Houses all stone + brick. It is situated on Grand River just above the mouth where it runs in the Arks River. Got corn near where we camp also a nice peice of beef stake from an Indian. Camp on bank of river as it is too late for us all to cross have to ferry it.

The military post was occupied from 1824 until 1857. It was used again as a military post during the Civil War and in 1863 was called Fort Blunt, after a Union army general. The post was abandoned in 1890.

The capitol of the Cherokee Nation at Tahlequah as it appeared in 1898. Construction of the building began about 1868, the year Jack Bailey passed through Tahlequah. Courtesy Western History Collections, University of Oklahoma Libraries.

Tuesday October th 27th 1868

We are at the river waiting to cross. Six or seven waggons have to crop [cross] first as they came first. There is several waggons on the other bank comeing this way. It will be 12 oclock before we can get off. Had a bad streak of luck last night. The dogs got all our meat. Another camp in same fix. Lao baked apples for breakfast. All siting around the landing. Sun two hours high. Nobody come to the ferry yet. The ferryman is an Indian a lazy son of a squaw. Here they come [*page 127*] at last. Across 12 oclock. Noon about one mile from ferry. We cross the river about a quarter mile below the mouth of Grand River. I suppose boats run up this far sometimes. The river is very

The main street in Fort Gibson, Cherokee Nation, in 1890, about twenty years after Jack Bailey passed through the area on his return journey to Texas. Courtesy Western History Collections, University of Oklahoma Libraries.

wide but the sand bars are too many and without the river is very full it is too shallow. I am told there is at this time a little boat at Gibson. There is three droves of cattle at this place trying to swim. One I am told has tryed 8 days in succession. Made it to day. Hired some Indians to assist them. The other swiming. One stear came by cam with 4 Indians after him. Cant drive him so they let in to shooting him. Soon killed him. They keep jus enough anyway. An Indian + a Negroe (both men) had a real old fist fight on the bank of the river. The Indian flaxed Mr Curly. We are once more on the prairie. Have been in timber so long that it makes me glad to see the prairie. (Daraty + family are still with us.[)] Find them to be clever folks. [*page 128*] Never overtaken Beadle yet. Hope we wont The young man that is traveling with Daraty eats so many apples, I gave him the name of Cider pres. We call him that all the time. In fact I dont know his right name. Once more on good road. Now we can travel faster. Came 10 miles to a creek. Struck camp for the night.

Wednesday October 28th 1868

Drove like thunder to day. Had a splendid road.[85] In the Creek Nation. Got a very early start. Met several droves of cattle from Texas going up into Missouri. Met Mr. Darnelle with a drove for Missouri. Another man from Denton. I dident learn his name bound for Arks. Two or three others for Missouri.[86] A regular built Yankee family camping near us to night on their way for McKiney Texas[87] I dont think he likes us much. We anoy him + more especially his wife + daughter [*page 129*] holering for Seymore. They are just moveing from Iowa. The old man has been liveing in Texas ever since

85. The "splendid road" ran south-southwest from Fort Gibson through the Creek Nation to North Fork Town and on to Boggy Depot, Nail's crossing, and Carriage Point, into the Chickasaw Nation and to Colbert's Ferry located on the Red River.

86. Bailey's journal leaves no doubt that in 1868, in spite of quarantine laws, Texas stock raisers were still driving their herds up the Shawnee Trail to Missouri and Arkansas.

87. McKinney, Texas, county seat of Collin County. McKinney is located about thirty miles south of Sherman, Texas.

the war. The man that is traveling with them says we are too rough a set for them and the old lady says she will be bound we are nothing but rebels. I wish she would say something to us about it. The old man + his son are Grant men dead out. You bet we give Grant thunder also all Rads. Got corn to night from a Creek Indian. He has a store + blacksmith shop. Several houses scatered around it. Has a name but I forgot to enquire what it is. The store + shop is on the right of the road. His house lots + garden on the left. Stoped to camp. Old Yank close to us. We made it hapen so he had to camp first so we got right close to him not over 20 steps and of all the holering singing dancing + cuting up generally we had it. The young man came over + tryed to laugh but it was mighty dry. At last his mama called him. The old lady looked dagers at me you bet.

[*page 130*] *Thursday October 29th 1868*

Got a daylight start this morning. Came 3 ½ miles to a large lake. ½ mile to north fork town. About 5 dry good stores 2 or three bakerys + a drug store. Got corn here for to night. Tom Christian + old Mc left us here. They concluded to go back. Heard of so many apples comeing to Texas that they would sell out here at $1 75/100) per bushel + git back. Came 6 miles to the Canadian River.[88] Camp near the river. Bone Christian is still with us. Old

88. Bailey and his party probably reached the Canadian River a few miles west of modern Stigler in Haskell County, Oklahoma.

Yank couldent get shet of us. Daraty with us yet. Old Yank tryed to dodge us at north fork town but we stuck to him. I aint done with him yet. It is so dark I close for the night.

Friday Octobe th 30th 1868

Another daylight start to day. We have eat our breakfast fed + geared up. Are waiting for daylight. I am scribbling by firelight [...] evening [...] passed over a tolerable rough road to day and one of the worst [*page 131*] hills imaginable. Called the Devils Back Bone had to pay 25 cts a waggon for going down it.[89] The road is chartered one mile. The fellow throwed some of the large rock out of the road. It is about three quarters of a mile down it and very steep + the boys along that passed over it before it was worked on say they dont mind paying their two bits. From the sign it must have been a dreadful place. 'Tis bad enough yet. Nooning on a branch where somebody camped last night. I think it was Cherokees layout as we met him soon this morning Fos has charge of the drove they are going to Abbaline Kansas. Met several movers all from Texas Some for Arks, some for Missouri some for Kansas. Came to Perryville in the Chocktaw Nation.[90]

89. The Devil's Backbone is not the prominent mountain of the same name running east and west to the south of Pocola in Le Flore County, Oklahoma, which is too far south of Bailey's 1868 route of travel. It is most likely a road near Beaver Mountain located just north of present-day Quinton in Haskell County, Oklahoma.

90. The site of Perryville is five miles southwest of McAlester, Oklahoma. Perryville, named for James Perry, an early resident, was an important community in

Has two stores both owned by Indians. Several houses. Not very fine one. Several Negro Camp. Have no houses to got to. Came out one mile camp on creek. Very thinly settled. Ever since we got in the Chocktaw Nation.

[*page 132*] *Sunday October the 31st 1868*

I suffered like thunder last night with rheumatism in my hand + harm. But all right this morning. There was two men passed our camp last night. They had been back horse hunting. They were moveing to Missouri. Couldent find their horses, (5 in number). They think the Indians got them. Nooning on creek. Have met several movers to day <u>We</u> <u>saw</u> <u>the</u> <u>old</u> <u>he</u> <u>Dr</u> Cole formely of Jacksboro notoriety.[91] Says that the d—n rebels are cuting up so in Texas it was not safe for a good <u>loyal</u> citizen to to live there. Says the rebs are giveing union men + negroes particular Jepee [*sp?*] There, (hope so) glory in their spunk, old Cole had about 50 head of cattle. Several head of old ponies + two of the funnyest aranged hacks or little waggons I or anybody else ever saw. His own build and patern. I never saw the like of travel [*page 133*] both ways in my life though I believe we see more moveing from than to Texas. I would give 50 dollars to be at home to night. Crosed another toll bridge to day. Take up for the night.

---

the Choctaw Nation before 1861. It was the site of a Civil War engagement in August 1863.

91. Efforts to identify Dr. Cole were unsuccessful. His name does not appear on the 1860 U.S. census for Jack County, Texas.

Monday November th 1st 1868

Got a very early start this morning. Met an old blind Indian beging. Her, husband was with. He a thundering big man. She dident get much from our crowd. We told her to put her old man to work. I gave her an apple or two. Bone gave the man a good cussing. Stoped to non on a branch. Came to another tool bridge. One mile this sid at the edge of prairie is a store. We sold 2 bushels apples. Took to bridge on Little Boggs. Came 11 miles to Boggy. Another bridge 1 mile. Came to Boggs Depot.[92] It is the oldest looking place I ever saw. A crowd of Negroes were gathered around th store which appeared to be the only one in town.[93] Saw very few white [*page 134*] men in town. Came out three miles to Dr. Thompson's.[94] Got corn + camped at carriage Point, if nothing hapens we camp in.

~~*Monday November 2nd*~~ [*date crossed out*]

~~Got a very early start this morning,~~ [*sentence crossed out*] Texas tomorrow. Young Yankee got his hand badly cut to day with the ketch of his bridle.

92. Boggy Depot is located fourteen miles southwest of Atoka in Atoka County, Oklahoma. Some Chickasaw Indians constructed a log cabin on the site in 1837. The settlement grew, and a post office was established there late in 1849. It was discontinued in 1944. Boggy Depot took its name from nearby Boggy Creek.

93. The store at Boggy Depot may have been the one established about 1860 by Reuben Wright from New England, but soon after the Civil War began Wright returned east. Who was operating the store in 1868 is not known.

94. Perhaps Giles Thompson, a wealthy Choctaw, who operated a salt works about three miles south of Boggy Depot. The title "doctor" may be an honorific because of Thompson's position in the community.

Jack Bailey probably traveled over the old stage line road that was the main street of Old Boggy Depot. This photograph of the road was made some years after Bailey traveled it. Courtesy Oklahoma Historical Society, Oklahoma City.

Tuesday Nov the 3d 1868

One thing I omited puting down Yesterday. We passed Naile's store + steam Mill on Blue a large creek.[95] They are building a large toll bridge.[96] Nearly every branch in the nation has got a toll bridge over it. The Yankee is still

95. The mill may have been one set up by a Captain Hester northeast of Boggy Depot for extracting and cleaning the seeds of bois d'are apples found in Boggy bottoms. The apples, commonly called hedge balls, were first crushed in the mill, the pulp running into a trough set in the swift water of the west branch of Boggy River, where the seeds were washed clean. The seeds were next removed, dried, sacked, and shipped to Fort Smith, Arkansas, then reshipped to distant points and sold for planting Osage-orange hedges, which at that time were used instead of fences on many western farms.

96. The toll bridge over the Boggy River a few miles northwest of Boggy Depot was established in 1866 by Capt. Charles LeFlore.

traveling near us. They asked us at the mill 8 cts per bbl for beef fresh.[97] Dident get it. Corn is selling along the road at $1 75/100 per bushel currency. Cross Red River to day noon at Culberts ferry, there is a little store on this bank (west bank).[98] [*page 135*] Cam on nearly on in two miles of Sherman. Camped for the night near a Negroe house. Boys dident get any of his chickins but some how we had four next morning for breakfast + I smelt feathers burning in the night. Got an early start came to Sherman.[99] Sold Bone's apples. Let him go home 15 miles from Sherman. He says, so we are done with him. Old Yank leaves us here. Came out 15 miles. Found no wood or water. Camped on prairie.

Wednesday Nov the 4th

Came about 4 miles to breakfast this morning. Get wood from a house a man named Kbert is with us now.

97. Perhaps a flourmill and cotton gin established by Allen Wright near Boggy Depot. It was the only mill in southern Indian Territory, and people living as far as seventy-five miles away would have their wheat ground here.

98. Colbert's Ferry was located on the Red River southwest of modern Colbert, Oklahoma, and north of present-day Denison, Texas. Joseph Mitchell, a Chickasaw, established a ferry at this point in 1842, but he died in 1847. About 1849 Benjamin Franklin Colbert arranged for Joseph B. Earhart to start another ferry at this point. In 1868 it was a popular crossing of the Red River and became known as Colbert's Ferry, a name also given to the small community that developed there.

99. Sherman, located in central Grayson County, Texas, south of Dennison, was established in 1846 and designated the county seat. Named for Gen. Sidney Sherman, a hero of the Texas Revolution, it had a population of 400 by 1852. The town grew and by the end of the 1860s had a population approaching 6,000.

He is on his way to Ft Griffen.[100] Got to Pilot Point sold out Hardens apples.[101] Sold some at 1 00 per bushel. [*page 136*] Hear lots of Indian news, see families geting futher. I never hear the like if I dident know better. I wouldent near go farther on the frontier but I have heard too much talk of this kind. One consolation the men at Pilot Point are going out + kill all the Indians. Joe Carol is at their head. He is first spokesman. I thought awhile they were going to pres us in to service. Darata leaves us here for home. The man that is with him goes on with us. Met a family from Denton runing from the Indians, tells an awful tale. Camp on Elm Creek.

Friday November the 6th

I have made a boble in the last two or three days. So near home + nothing transpireing worthy of note that I have become carles. Sunday we came through Boggy [*page 137*] Depot. Monday through Carriage Point. Tuesday crossed Red River. Wednesday passed through Sherman. Thursday got to Pilot Point where we lightened our load of apples. In fact sold out all but a few for home consumption. Now

100. Fort Griffin was established in west Texas as Camp Wilson in 1867. Its name was soon changed to Fort Griffin. It is located near the town of Albany northeast of Abilene, Texas. Fort Griffin, once called the "wickedest town in the West," lasted until 1881. The site is today a Texas state park.

101. Pilot Point, Texas, was about eighteen miles north of Denton in northeastern Denton County. It received its name from a grove of oak trees with one tall cottonwood tree that served as a landmark for Indians, Texas Rangers, and pioneers. A settlement was platted there early in 1854 and a post office was established in 1855 at James D. Walcott's general store. Following the Civil War in 1866 Pilot Point was incorporated.

Friday here we are. Stoped to noon n Denton creek.[102] Cme about 22 miles to day. Got good scared to day. We saw 75 or 100 head of horses. Thought they wer Indian horses + all the cattle we could see were running. Looked Scottish you bet. I was glad when we found out what it was. Every body left this part of the country. Passed several vacant houses. In fact all we passed were vacant. Only three familys in Boliver. They were fixing to leave. We are trying to get to Decatur to day. Got to Decatur nearly night. Put up at Mrs Perrins. Found every [*page 138*] body in a stir about Indians. Several puting up with Perrins as a protection to families.[103]

Saturday November 7th 1868

Leave for home this morning. Jim stops here. I have got Dobbs + Albert with me yet. Get a late start. Noon at Prairie Point.[104] Came out in one mile of west fork. Camp for the night. Here Dodge leaves us. I am glad to get rid of

102. Denton Creek is located in Montague County, Texas. It rises four miles northwest of Bowie, Texas, and then runs southeast for thirty-two miles through Wise and Denton Counties in Texas. The creek was named for John B. Denton.

103. Decatur, Texas, the county seat of Wise County, is forty miles northwest of Fort Worth near the western edge of the Grand Prairies and near the western Cross Timbers. The town, first called Taylorsville and named for Gen. Zachary Taylor, was laid out about 1856. Early in 1858 it was renamed Decatur for the naval hero Stephen Decatur. Bailey, learning that Indians had killed several settlers in Parker County, sought the safety of Decatur, Texas, on his journey home. Mrs. Perrin of Decatur, Texas, may have been Mrs. L. W. Perrin, whose son Louis founded Perrin, Texas, in nearby Jack County about 1870.

104. Prairie Point was located in southeastern Wise County, Texas, near modern Rhome, Texas. Prairie Point was established in the late 1850s by

him. His mother lives about 5 miles from here. I was in hopes we would get home to night but cant make it.

Sunday November 8th 1868

Get a day light start. Cross west fork at mouth of Indian Creek. Noon in six miles of home. Passed through Veals Station.[105] [*page 139*] Got home before sundown. Now you have my travels to Kansas + back home. I have left out some things that I wish I had put in but my paper run short before I got to Kansas. I dont force you to read this so if you dont like it, just lay it down + dont critisize me for I make no pretintions toward writeing or any thing of the kind. Hope it will interest some people.

Respectfully
Jack Bailey

[*page 140*]

When Gus swaped old Gray off some of the boys asked me to compose a piece of poetry on old gray, here it is..

Missourians at the junction of two stagecoach lines about twelve miles southeast of Decatur, Texas.

105. Veal's Station is located twelve miles north of Weatherford, Texas, in northeastern Parker County. Among the first settlers who arrived in the early 1850s was William G. Veal, who opened a general store. Postal service began in 1857, but the community developed slowly because of an almost continuous Indian threat. Postal service was discontinued in 1868. After Indians were driven from the area by the mid-1870s, the community began to grow. By the mid-1880s Veal's Station was a farming center with about a hundred residents, a school, three churches, and a general store.

Old Gray is gone Gus swaped him off
Twas not because he had a cough
The old fellow's back it got so sore
Gus swore he wouldent ride him more

Once on a time old Gray was good
Because he always got the food
But now old Gray has got so poor
Gus swore he wouldent ride him more

Good by old Gray we mis you so
Though it took spurs + quirt to make you go
You walked so game til you got poor
Gus swears he'll never ride you more

[page 141]
He let you go for a little mare
The way he swaped was hardly fare
Just like he thought you were no account
But you was alway ready when he went to mount

Your little head it looked so neat
We admire your neck we admire your feet
And then your body is so round
Your belly almost drags the ground

Once more good bye we mis that neigh
We hope to see you another day

And hope your back will not be sore
Then Gus will wish he could ride you more[106]

[page 142]

Gus traded for a saddle upon which the following was made in camp by one of the boys, also a fine bridle.

Gus Hendley traded for a saddle
upon which he rides astraddle
A bridle too I realy swear
To put upon his old gray mare

Go on Gus I wish you well
Although you have not cows to sell
You have traded 'till your'e traded out
But with the old gray mare you can dash about

Put you riging on your mare
We love to see her pitch and rare
If you dont watch she'll run away
And then you'll wish you had old Gray

[page 143]

You will wish the old gray mare in hell
The saddle and bridle you are sure to sell

106. The placement of this poem near the end of the journal suggests that Bailey wrote down his words about Gus Hendley's experiences from memory after his return to Parker County, Texas.

To some one that will never pay
And then you will call for good old Gray
Finis

-

No man can be happy if self is the sole objects of his thoughts and wishes.

No man can be happy if conscience tells him that he has left a single duty unperformed.

-

[page 146]

Distance's course + continued from the first leaf in book

20"	day travel	north	5 miles
21"	" "	"	10 miles
22"	" "	"	8 miles
23"	" "	"	15 "
24"	" "	"	8 "
25"	" "	"	8 "
26"	" "	east of north	3 "
27"	" "	"	12 "
28"	" "	"	9 "
29"	" "	"	10 "
30"	" "	"	6 "
31"	" "	"	6 "
32"	" "	"	6 "
33"	" "	"	9 "
34"	" "	N of W	9 "
35"	" "	"	10 "
36"	" "	"	4 "

This is to Walnut Creek 110 miles this side of Abalaine, the course from that point is a little west of North[107]

[page 147]

Lines on giveing up a ring that was given as a token of love, and engagement

You say I must give up this thing
And though 'tis nothing but a ring
It makes my heart feel sore + sad
I hate to give it up so bad

107. After returning to Texas, Bailey apparently used the information in his journal to calculate the distances he traveled beginning on the twentieth day of his trail drive. That he begins on the twentieth day and not the first suggests that he either did not keep a journal for the first twenty days or had somehow lost or destroyed the journal's opening pages before returning to Texas. Bailey calculated that between the vicinity of Fort Arbuckle in southern Indian Territory and the Walnut River in southern Kansas, he traveled a distance of 138 miles. The distance he covered, however, is more like 180 miles when calculated on a modern map. Bailey's estimate of the miles covered does not appear accurate. Since his journal begins on the twentieth day of the trail drive, it seems that the herd took twenty days to travel from some point in north Texas across the Red River to near Fort Arbuckle. The distance from the Red River to Fort Arbuckle is about sixty miles and would have required about eight days of travel. Subtracting eight days from the twenty days used to reach Fort Arbuckle, they probably traveled about twelve days from the herd's starting point to the Red River, less at least one day to get the cattle across the stream. That leaves eleven days of travel in Texas. Since Bailey and the others on the drive probably knew the terrain in north Texas and might average ten miles a day with their herd, the drive probably started at some point about a hundred miles south of the Red River. They most likely started from Parker, Wise, or Jack Counties in Texas. It is estimated that Jack Bailey's journey by horseback from Texas to Kansas and back actually covered about 635 miles.

You spoke as though we traded,
And 'twas not a token true,
I took it as a gift of love
But I give it back to you

Tis not because I love you less
Oh no my dearest wife
Why tear this gift of love from me
Tis dear to me as life

But then tis yours I give it up
No matter how I feel
But Mat I love you better now
When our engagement this did seal

[page 148]

Many pleasant hours of love
Amid life's dreary ways by Jove
The time has come my little wife
That we have to lead a diferent life

In old age we are fast progrissing
Even you as both's confesing
But why should we our age complain
Amid our trials can be young again

In every trial let us both agree
Love is all then pray love me
End of time will come at last

You must I beg pass time off fast
Jack Bailey

Even you are growing old
Very soon you'll be a scold
Then we all must hunt our hole
How many times you've tried to marry
You smiled at boys like a little fairry
[...] will be you'll discard Harry[108]

108. This poem by Bailey, apparently written to his wife, suggests that he may have experienced marital problems before leaving on the trail drive to Kansas. When he wrote the poem is not known.

Bibliography

Ancestry.com. http://www.ancestry.com.

Brayer, Herbert O., editor. *Life of Tom Candy Ponting, An Autobiography*. Evanston, Ill.: Branding Iron Press, 1952.

Church of Jesus Christ of Latter-day Saints. Family Search. http://www.familysearch.org

Cox, James. *Historical and Biographical Record of the Cattle Industry and the Cattlemen of Texas and Adjacent Territory*. St. Louis: Woodward & Tiernan Printing Co., 1895.

Cutler, William G. *History of the State of Kansas*. Chicago: Andreas, 1882.

Dale, Edward Everett. *The Range Cattle Industry*. Norman: University of Oklahoma Press, 1930.

Dary, David. *Cowboy Culture: A Saga of Five Centuries*. New York: Alfred A. Knopf, 1981.

———. *Lawrence, Douglas County, Kansas: An Informal History*. Lawrence: Allen Books, 1982.

Duffield, George Crawford. "Driving Cattle from Texas to Iowa, 1866." *Annals of Iowa* 14 (1924).

Freeman, James W., editor. *Prose and Poetry of the Livestock Industry of the United States . . .* Kansas City, Mo.: Franklin Hudson Publishing Co., 1905.

Gordon, Clarence W. "Report on Cattle, Sheep, and Swine, Supplementary to Enumeration of Live Stock on Farms in 1880." In *Report on the Production of Agriculture. Tenth*

Census. Vol. 3. Washington, D.C.: Department of Interior, 1883.

History of the Cattlemen of Texas. A Brief Resume of the Live Stock Industry of the Southwest and a Biographical Sketch of Many of the Important Characters Whose Lives Are Interwoven Therein. Dallas: Johnston Printing and Advertising Co., 1914.

Hunter, J. Marvin, compiler and editor. *The Trail Drivers of Texas*. 2 vols. San Antonio: Jackson Printing Co., 1920, 1923, 1924. Vol. 1 was corrected and reissued in 1924.

Kansas Atlas & Gazetteer. Yarmouth, Me.: DeLorne Publishing Co., 1997.

McCoy, Joseph. *History Sketches of the Cattle Trade of the West and Southwest*. Kansas City, Mo.: Ramsey, Millett & Hudson, 1874.

Morris, John W., Charles R. Goins, and Edwin C. McReynolds. *Historical Atlas of Oklahoma*. 3d ed. Norman: University of Oklahoma Press, 1986.

Morris, Lerona Rosamond, editor. *Oklahoma Yesterday-Today-Tomorrow*. Guthrie: Co-Operative Publishing Co.,1930.

Oklahoma Atlas & Gazetteer. Yarmouth, Me.: DeLorme Publishing Co., 1998.

Paddock, B. B. *History of Texas; Fort Worth and the Texas Northwest*. 3 vols. Chicago: Lewis Publishing Co., 1922.

Ponting, Tom Candy. "The Man and His Recollections." *Decatur* (Illinois) *Review*, 9, 16, 23 June 1907. Published in three parts.

Randolph, Vance. *Ozark Folksongs*. 4 vols. Columbia: State Historical Society of Missouri, 1946–50.

Shirk, George H. *Oklahoma Place Names*. Norman: University of Oklahoma Press, 1965.

Skaggs, Jimmy M. *The Cattle-Trailing Industry between Supply and Demand 1866–1890*. Lawrence: University of Kansas Press, 1973.

Socolofsky, Homer E., and Huber Self. *Historical Atlas of Kansas*. Norman: University of Oklahoma Press, 1975.

Taylor, Lonn. *The American Cowboy*. New York: Harper & Row, 1983.

Todd, O. H. "With the Early Surveyors of Indian Territory." In *Michigan Engineers' Annual*. Battle Creek, Mich.: Press of the Review and Herald Publishing Co., n.d. [1899].

Tyler, Ron, editor. *The New Handbook of Texas*. 6 vols. Austin: Texas State Historical Association, 1996. Available online.

U.S. Census. Census rolls (1860, 1870, 1880) for Jack, Wise, Denton, Montague, Cooke, Parker, and Tarrant Counties, Texas. Census rolls (1870) for Lyon County, Kansas. Texas tax rolls (1958 and 1959) for Jack County, Texas. Available online at Census Finder:
http://www.censusfinder.com/index.htm

Wright, Muriel H. "Old Boggy Depot." *Chronicles of Oklahoma* 5, no. 1 (March 1927).

Index

www.ingramcontent.com/pod-product-compliance
Ingram Content Group UK Ltd.
Pitfield, Milton Keynes, MK11 3LW, UK
UKHW041323190726
13851UKWH00013B/72

9 780806 146478